PHILIPPINES

The killing goes on

AI Index: ASA/35/01/92

ISBN: 0 86210 201 1

First published February 1992

Amnesty International
Publications
1 Easton Street
London WC1X 8DJ
United Kingdom

Printed by:
Flashprint Enterprises Ltd.

Original language English

CONTENTS

ABBREVIATIONS

ADLO-CL	— Alliance of Democratic Labor Organizations-Central Luzon
AFP	— Armed Forces of the Philippines
CAFGU	— Citizen Armed Force Geographical Unit
CAPCOM	— Capital Regional Command
CHDF	— Civilian Home Defense Force
CHR	— Commission on Human Rights
CPLA	— Cordillera People's Liberation Army
CPP	— Communist Party of the Philippines
CVO	— Citizen Volunteer Organization
DATC	— Development Agency of Tribes in the Cordillera
DND	— Department of National Defense
EO	— Executive Order
FLAG	— Free Legal Assistance Group
IB	— Infantry Battalion
ICCPR	— International Covenant on Civil and Political Rights
INP	— Integrated National Police
KADENA	— *Kabatan para sa Demokrasya at Nasyonalismo* (Youth for Democracy and Nationalism)
KMP	— *Kilusang Magbubukid ng Pilipinas* (Peasant Movement of the Philippines)
KMU	— *Kilusang Mayo Uno* (May First Movement)
MNLF	— Moro National Liberation Front
NBI	— National Bureau of Investigation
NDF	— National Democratic Front
NFSW	— National Federation of Sugar Workers
NPA	— New People's Army
PAHRA	— Philippine Alliance of Human Rights Advocates
PC	— Philippine Constabulary
PCPR	— Promotion of Church People's Rights
PD	— Presidential Decree
PCHR	— Presidential Committee on Human Rights
PHRC	— Presidential Human Rights Committee
PIC	— Philippine Independent Church
PLLP	— Protestant Lawyers League of the Philippines
PNP	— Philippine National Police
PSG	— Presidential Security Group
RA	— Republic Act
RAM	— Reform the Armed Forces Movement, also *Rebolusyonaryong Alyansa Makabansa* (Revolutionary Alliance of the Masses)
SIKLAB	— A workers' cultural group
SOT	— Special Operation Team
TFDP	— Task Force Detainees of the Philippines
UCCP	— United Church of Christ in the Philippines
UN	— United Nations
WPD	— Western Police District

The Philippines

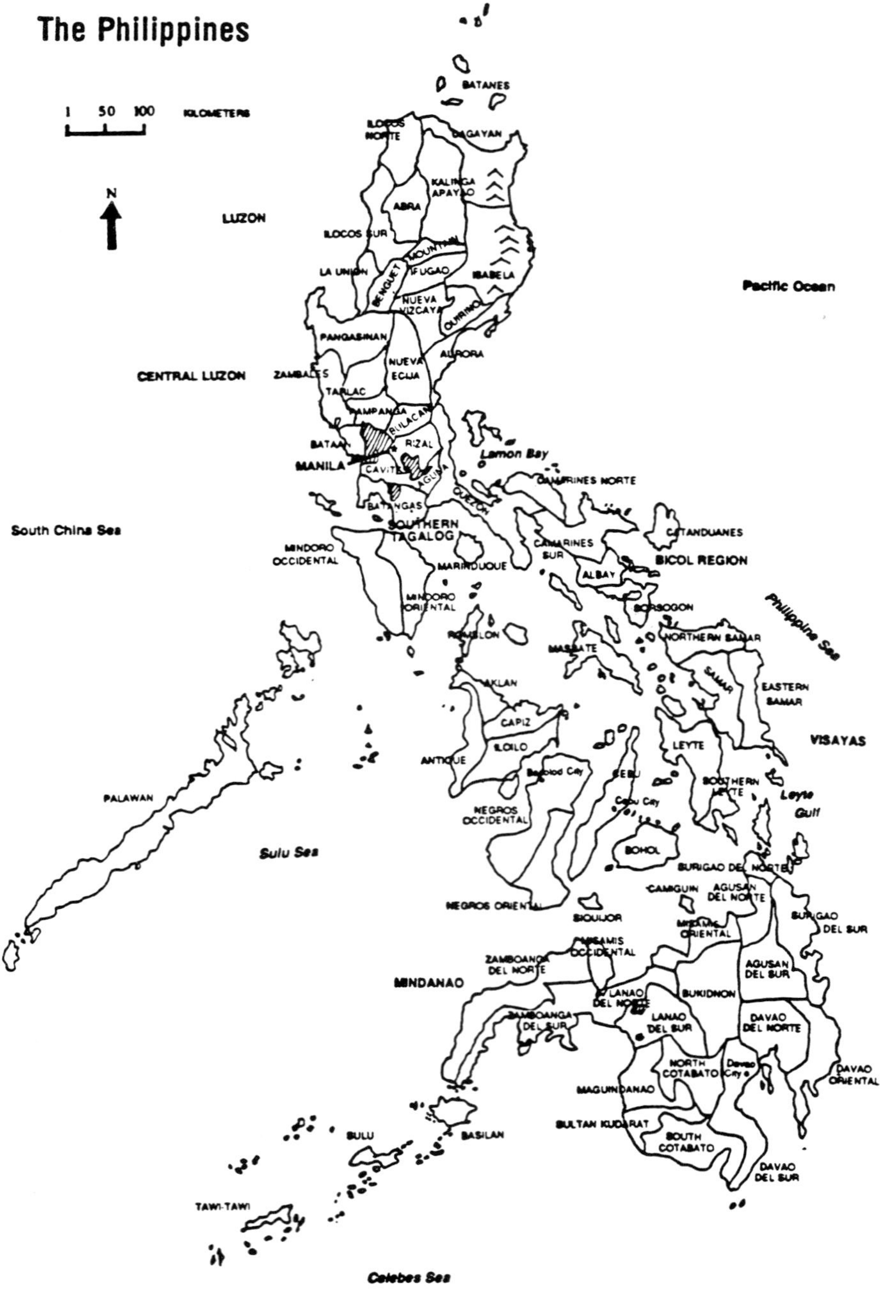

INTRODUCTION

Since 1988 at least 550 people, all of them unarmed, have been killed by government or government-backed forces in the Philippines. The authorities have frequently sought to portray the victims as legitimate targets in their long-running campaign to defeat armed opposition groups. But the facts tell a different story. Whole families have been gunned down. Villagers working in their fields have been shot dead. Women have been raped by gangs of soldiers before being killed. The most inhuman forms of torture, including castration, have been inflicted on people targeted for death. No section of society has escaped, although the socially and economically disadvantaged and the politically weak have been the most vulnerable. The armed opposition has also been responsible for political killings. The victims have included residents of rural communities, trade unionists, government officials and opposition group members suspected of spying for the military.

The likelihood of an improvement in the government's human rights record increased in 1986, when Corazon Aquino was swept into office on the back of the "People's Power revolution" against then President Ferdinand Marcos. Democracy was formally restored and the new government promised to make a clean break with the policies and practices of the government of President Marcos, whose regime had become a byword for human rights violations. Yet within two years Amnesty International had published the first in a series of reports showing that political killings were being committed on a large scale and that they had become the most serious human rights problem in the country.[1] This report shows the extent to which the killings go on.

Those responsible for extrajudicial executions have included members of the Philippine

Army (PA), the Philippine Constabulary (PC), the Integrated National Police (INP) the newly formed Philippine National Police (PNP), militia units known as Citizen Armed Force Geographical Units (CAFGU), and authorized civilian groups known as Civilian Volunteer Self-Defense Organizations (CVOs). Also involved have been semi-official and unofficial paramilitary groups, including anti-communist vigilante groups known to function with the acquiescence of, or in collusion with, formal security forces.

Some of the killings have been particularly brutal. In July 1989 two women suspected of belonging to an armed opposition group were killed after being arrested by a group of 50 soldiers and CAFGU members. After being tied and kicked by the soldiers, the commanding captain slashed and stabbed the women's ears with a hunting knife. Both women were raped by more than half of the group of armed men. The next day they were stabbed to death and buried near a river.

A man detained at a military checkpoint in February 1990 was later found dead. Police said he had been shot when he had tried to grab a gun while under arrest. An autopsy revealed that he had been shot 28 times and that his arms had been broken. The back of his head was shattered and wounds indicated that bullets had been fired near his genitals.

Many of those killed have been children, including infants and the very elderly. On 3 August 1990, 19 members of a Muslim family were lined up outside their home and shot dead by soldiers. The victims included a pregnant woman, six children aged between one and 13 years and two of the children's grandparents. The soldiers claimed they had come to arrest a member of the family who was suspected of being a Muslim rebel.

Extrajudicial executions are part of a broader pattern of serious human rights violations in the Philippines. Hundreds of people have "disappeared" in police or military custody since 1986 and a significant number of the "disappeared" are known to have been killed or tortured. The practice of "disappearance" itself contributes to the incidence of arbitrary killing and torture. People held in unacknowledged, secret detention, without access to family or lawyers, are particularly at risk of being killed or tortured. The risks are intensified in situations, such as that in the Philippines, where police or military forces feel free to commit such violations without fear of punishment.[2]

Amnesty International has also documented other serious

Those living in rural areas have figured prominently among the hundreds of people who have been killed by government or government-backed forces in recent years. Many have been killed by military or paramilitary units while working in their fields. Others have died when their homes have been strafed by soldiers using automatic weapons: the traditional wood and bamboo housing offers little resistance to bullets. Bodies of villagers taken away for "questioning" have been found dumped in rivers or by roadsides, often bearing signs of torture. © Carol Lee human rights violations in the Philippines. In 1991 there were at least 12 known prisoners of conscience and possibly many more among hundreds of political prisoners. Scores of political detainees have alleged that they have been tortured or ill-treated while held in custody for investigation. In 1990 and 1991 leading military and government figures endorsed moves to restore the death penalty for so-called heinous crimes, including political offences such as rebellion and subversion.[3]

This report focuses on extrajudicial executions and complements previous reports which have detailed "disappearance" and torture in the Philippines. The report describes the pattern of killings between 1988 and 1991. It shows how particular groups of people, such as trade unionists, human rights lawyers, religious leaders and peasant activists, have been targeted. It includes case studies of 85 people who were killed by government or government-backed forces, and of several others killed by armed opposition groups. The report examines why these killings have continued in the Philippines despite the early attempts by the new government to promote and protect human rights. It also offers a set of recommendations which, if implemented, would help to put a stop to political killings and other violations of basic human rights.

The killings and why they continue

Extrajudicial executions in the Philippines have occurred against the background of more than two decades of violent political conflict between government forces and a variety of armed opposition groups. The most important of these have been the New People's Army (NPA) — the armed wing of the Communist Party of the Philippines (CPP) — and the Moro National Liberation Front (MNLF). Military and government authorities have frequently portrayed the victims of human rights violations as legitimate targets in their counter-insurgency campaign and have treated political killings as the inevitable by-product of the armed conflict. Moreover, they have sought to justify this position — and in so doing to relieve the security forces of responsibility for human rights violations — by pointing out that armed opposition groups have themselves committed human rights abuses.

Amnesty International recognizes that the government faces a serious threat from armed opposition groups, and it condemns human rights abuses committed by such groups. However, abuses by opposition groups are never a justification for governments to disregard their obligations to respect fundamental rights. In attempting to retreat from or ignore these obligations, the Philippine authorities have helped to perpetuate the problem of extrajudicial execution, rather than to solve it. They have also contributed to a political climate in which opposition groups themselves are more likely to resort to acts of violence and human rights abuse.

The persistence of serious human rights violations is, to some extent, a consequence of the long-standing influence of the military within the Philippine political system. In spite of the formal restoration of democracy in 1986 and the principle of civilian supremacy enshrined in the 1987 Constitution, the military has maintained a dominant role in the political life of the nation under President Aquino's administration. Patterns of military behaviour which were institutionalized under the dictatorship of former President Marcos have continued, including systematic human rights violations. Military authorities have consistently stymied genuine human rights initiatives at the implementation stage, portraying them as the efforts of "subversives" or "communists" intent only on sullying the reputation of the military for impure or dubious political ends. The civilian government has appeared unable, and at times unwilling, to exert the necessary political will to ensure that human rights initiatives are properly implemented.

The present government has reinforced the dominance of the military by giving it considerable autonomy and freedom of action in conducting the counter-insurgency campaign. Aspects of this campaign have contributed significantly to the problem of extrajudicial execution. Paramount among these are:

- the practice of "red-labelling" or targeting alleged critics and opponents of the government as "subversives" or NPA/CPP sympathizers;
- the creation of and reliance on an ever-widening network of official militia and semi-official paramilitary forces which are poorly trained and undisciplined.

The practice of "red-labelling" has increasingly placed members of lawful non-governmental organizations at risk of extrajudicial execution, "disappearance" and arbitrary arrest. The use of poorly trained and undisciplined militia and paramilitary forces in combatting the insurgency has inevitably contributed to the incidence of extrajudicial executions and other serious violations.

Members of government and government-backed forces responsible for extrajudicial executions have been able to commit such crimes with impunity. Of the hundreds of political killings reported since 1986, only a handful have been properly investigated and the perpetrators have almost never been brought to justice. Two of those convicted were low-ranking members of the police; the rest were former members of militia forces or civilian hitmen.

The ineffectiveness of the existing legal and institutional mechanisms for bringing perpetrators to justice stems largely from direct and indirect obstruction by the security forces which are the subject of investigations and prosecutions. Methods of obstruction include the intimidation of witnesses, complainants, lawyers, prosecutors and judges; and the refusal to provide investigating authorities access to information, personnel or military premises. Moreover, investigations are often conducted by staff belonging to the military or police units believed responsible for the violations. Inevitably the investigations lack rigour and impartiality and they rarely result in prosecution or conviction.

There are also serious flaws in the methods of work and mandate of the various civilian bodies — including the governmental Commission on Human Rights (CHR) and the civil courts — charged with investigation and prosecution. Partly because of pressure from the military and police, many civilian judicial and quasi-judicial bodies have come to operate according to a set of principles which, in effect, provide considerable leeway to the military, while creating difficulties for the victims or complainants. An additional problem has been the lack of clarity in defining the respective responsibilities of the various investigative and prosecutorial agencies. Overlapping authority and lack of clarity have meant that, all too often, none of the institutions takes full responsibility for resolving a case.

Since 1986 Amnesty International has repeatedly appealed to the government of President Aquino to address the continuing pattern of serious human rights violations. The government has noted Amnesty International's concerns and has acknowledged that some human rights violations have occurred, including extrajudicial executions. It has said that these constituted isolated incidents which ran counter to government policy. Government representatives have also pointed out that human rights violations are prohibited by Philippine law and the 1987 Constitution.

Amnesty International recognizes that there are substantial legal and institutional mechanisms available for the protection of human rights in the Philippines. However, as this report shows, aspects of government policy and military strategy have helped to perpetuate a climate in which extrajudicial executions and other serious human rights violations are likely to occur. Moreover, by its acceptance of and reliance upon seriously deficient procedures for investigating violations and bringing the perpetrators to justice, the government has failed to fulfil its responsibilities under domestic and international law and has created the impression that members of the security forces are beyond the reach of the law.

Urgent action is needed by the government to make it clear that violations of human rights will not be tolerated under any circumstances. The security forces must be held accountable for their actions, and for those of militia units or paramilitary groups operating under their command or with their acquiescence. Paramilitary groups, private armies and the CAFGU militia force must be dismantled. Procedures for investigating human rights violations and prosecuting those responsible must be radically revised so that the perpetrators of such crimes no longer feel they can act with impunity. In particular, witnesses, complainants and investigators in human rights cases must be given proper protection from harassment and threats. Until such action is taken by the government, the killings will undoubtedly go on.

1

Responsibility for the killings

What is an extrajudicial execution?

Amnesty International uses the term extrajudicial execution to describe unlawful and deliberate killings of real or alleged political opponents by governments, as well as killings instigated by government officials, or committed with their acquiescence. Extrajudicial executions are distinguished from necessary measures of law enforcement or acts of armed conflict. They are not accidental or "panic" killings by law enforcement officials and do not include killings which occur as a direct and unintended consequence of armed combat, for example, the killing of civilians in cross-fire. However, Amnesty International does define as extrajudicial execution the deliberate killing of unarmed civilians during military encounters. Deliberate killings of people held in custody are also considered to be extrajudicial executions.

Who is responsible?

Few governments admit to having a policy of killing political opponents. Yet even where there is no such declared policy, governments and military authorities should be held accountable for killings by their security forces if, through their statements, their acts or their failure to act, they appear to tolerate, condone or encourage the practice. Government and military authorities are also responsible for killings committed by unofficial or paramilitary forces where these operate with the support, knowledge or acquiescence of the official security forces.

Establishing direct responsibility for a particular extrajudicial execution in the Philippines can be difficult. Those believed responsible have attempted to conceal their identities or have subsequently claimed that the victim was killed in an armed encounter or while attempting to escape. Military and paramilitary operatives have carried out killings at night or in remote locations which make discovery of their unlawful activities unlikely. They have dressed in plainclothes, making identification more difficult. Victims have been killed after being arrested or have "disappeared" after being detained by government or government-backed forces; they have been taken to "safehouses" (unofficial detention centres) and interrogated before being executed. The bodies of such victims have frequently been dumped on the roadside, sometimes far from home. In these cases, members of the security forces have claimed that the victims had been released or had escaped from custody before they died.

In spite of such difficulties, there are at least three ways to establish a plausible case for culpability. First, eye-witnesses may identify the perpetrators by name. Second, eye-witnesses may identify property of the perpetrators, such as a vehicle, a weapon or a military insignia on a uniform. Third, when a person dies in police or military custody, or the body of the victim is found, an autopsy may establish the cause of death.

The government's obligations

The right to life is fundamental and protection of this right is enshrined in all major international human rights treaties and declarations.[4] Extrajudicial executions by members of the security forces, or by unofficial forces acting with their cooperation, are in clear violation of international human rights law.

Article 6 of the International Covenant on Civil and Political Rights (ICCPR) states that:

> *"Every human being has the inherent right to life. This right shall be protected by law. No one shall be arbitrarily deprived of his life."*

The ICCPR further specifies that the right not to be arbitrarily deprived of life must be upheld at all times and in all circumstances. Article 4 states that this right cannot be waived "even in times of public emergency threatening the life of the nation". The Human Rights Committee, in its general comment 6.6 on Article 6 of the ICCPR, has indicated that the right to life "should not be interpreted narrowly" and has emphasized the need for governments to take measures not only to prevent and punish deprivation of life by criminal acts, but also "to prevent arbitrary killing by their own security forces".

The obligations of states to protect the right to life are far-reaching. States which have ratified international treaties are bound not only to respect the right to life in principle, but to take effective measures to ensure that extrajudicial executions do not occur in practice. Principle 1 of the Principles on the Effective Prevention and Investigation of Extra-Legal, Arbitrary and Summary Executions, endorsed by the UN General Assembly in 1989, states that:

> *"Governments shall prohibit by law all extra-legal, arbitrary and summary executions and shall ensure that any such executions are recognized as offences under their criminal laws and are punishable by appropriate penalties, which take into account the seriousness of such offences".*

States party to the ICCPR are also obliged, under Article 2(3) a) and b), to ensure that remedies are available to the victims of human rights violations and that those remedies are effective. A government's obligations with respect to extrajudicial executions therefore extend to ensuring that investigations are thorough and impartial and that the suspected perpetrators are brought to justice.

The Philippine Government, which has ratified the ICCPR, has recognized these obligations. Under the 1987 Constitution the country adopted "...the generally accepted principles of international law as part of the law of the land..." (Section 2, Article II).[5] In response to a question from the Human Rights Committee in April 1989 concerning this section of the Constitution, the Philippine Government representative stated clearly that "the provisions of [the ICCPR] can be invoked before and directly enforced by Philippine courts and appropriate bodies". The rights and freedoms set out in the ICCPR are also enshrined in the Philippine Bill of Rights, Article III of the Constitution.[6]

Killings in a context of armed opposition

The risk of arbitrary killings is greatly increased during periods of armed conflict. Normal legal procedures are likely to be weakened or ignored by the authorities. The protection of human rights may be undermined by, or subordinated to, what are seen as the exigencies of national security. Members of the security forces, and others acting with their support, may feel free to commit human rights violations with impunity.

Amnesty International recognizes that armed opposition groups can present governments with particular difficulties in the maintenance of order and political stability. When an armed opposition group gains control over population or territory, and the government launches a counter-insurgency campaign to combat it, the possibility of violence being inflicted on unarmed or defenceless civilians inevitably arises. Under these conditions the conduct of both governments and insurgent forces is governed by humanitarian law as set out within Article 3, common to the four Geneva Conventions.[7] Article 3 establishes minimum humane standards for situations of internal armed conflict. It is applicable to both parties involved in a conflict, regardless of whether the other has agreed to be guided by its terms and standards.

The people to whom protection is extended under common Article 3 are defined as follows:

"Persons taking no active part in the hostilities,

© Carol Lee

Members of the Armed Forces of the Philippines on parade, Independence Day 1990. The military still plays a dominant political role in the Philippines under President Corazon Aquino's administration. Patterns of behaviour institutionalized under the dictatorship of former President Ferdinand Marcos have continued, including systematic and widespread violations of human rights. On average more than 100 people a year have been summarily killed by government or government-backed forces for political reasons since 1988. Hundreds of others have "disappeared" in police or military custody.

including members of armed forces who have laid down their arms and those placed hors de combat by sickness, wounds, detention, or any other cause...".

It prohibits "at any time and in any place whatsoever with respect to the above mentioned persons:

a) violence to life and person, in particular murder of all kinds, mutilation, cruel treatment and torture;
b) taking of hostages;
c) outrages upon personal dignity, in particular humiliating and degrading treatment;
d) the passing of sentences and the carrying out of executions without previous judgment pronounced by a regularly constituted court, affording all the judicial guarantees which are recognized as indispensable by civilized peoples".

All parties to the armed conflict in the Philippines have an obligation to uphold the terms of common Article 3 of the Geneva Conventions, and in particular to refrain from summary or

© Carol Lee

Members of the New People's Army (NPA), Negros, 1990. The NPA, the armed wing of the Communist Party of the Philippines, was formed in 1969. It has been engaged in armed opposition to the Philippine government since then. The largest armed opposition group, it was estimated by the Philippine authorities in 1987 to have around 25,000 members, although this number is believed to have declined since then. The NPA has been responsible for human rights abuses, including killings of trade unionists, members of the civilian administration, and people living in rural communities.

arbitrary executions at all times and under all circumstances.

Governments, however, are also bound to respect international law. They have a unique responsibility for upholding and protecting the human rights of the citizens falling within their jurisdiction and have at their disposal the full range of institutions, laws and resources with which to carry out their duties. For example, they are responsible for the conduct of the security forces and for ensuring that those believed to have committed human rights violations are brought to justice.

It is for these reasons, among others, that Amnesty International believes that the actions of armed opposition groups, however widespread and violent, can never be used to justify human rights violations by government forces or others acting with their cooperation. If governments show contempt for human rights, others may feel free to do likewise.

Moreover, if representatives of the state or its branches are permitted to act outside the framework of the law it is unlikely that human rights abuses in general will stop. In practice, it is only through prompt and impartial investigation of all reported killings that there can be any hope of bringing the perpetrators to justice and providing an effective framework for the prevention of future killings. When governments fail to investigate reported extrajudicial executions on the grounds that they might have been committed by opposition forces, or because the identities of the perpetrators are not immediately known, they effectively condone the practice of unlawful killing by their own agents or others acting with their consent or cooperation.

2

The Context

The Marcos years

The current pattern of human rights violations emerged during the government of former President Ferdinand Marcos. During his 20-year rule, and in particular after the declaration of martial law in September 1972, the violation of human rights was both systematic and brutal.[8] A climate conducive to the violation of basic human rights was created through the expansion of the power of the armed forces and the executive. Both facilitated arbitrary arrest and detention and military immunity from prosecution in civilian courts.

Political suspects who were arrested and detained during these years had few means of protecting themselves. There was no right of *habeas corpus* and the government was not legally obliged to bring detainees to trial. This situation facilitated other human rights violations. Torture was used widely and systematically by the security forces, particularly during what was termed "tactical interrogation" of suspects immediately following arrest. "Disappearances" and extrajudicial executions increased dramatically during the last five years of the Marcos government after martial law was officially lifted in 1981. Victims included politicians, lawyers, priests, church workers, journalists and students, all suspected of engaging in or supporting subversive activities. In some cases killings or "disappearances" were alleged to have been carried out by regular units of the armed forces. In others, militia organizations such as the Civilian Home Defense Forces (CHDF) and anti-communist vigilante groups acting with the support or cooperation of the military, were held responsible.

In the period of martial law between 1972

and 1981 the size and resources of the armed forces were substantially expanded. The relationship between the civilian government and the military forces also changed. Civilian authority over military forces was largely disregarded in practice, particularly in the provinces. The official justification for military expansion was the need to combat a growing insurgency and the guerrilla tactics of armed opposition groups. A side-effect of the expansion, however, was an increase in human rights violations by the military, which in turn increased popular support for insurgent w2groups.

Armed opposition

The Communist Party of the Philippines (CPP) was founded in December 1968 when a group of university students, heavily influenced by Maoism, broke away from the Stalinist *Partido Komunista ng Pilipinas* (PKP). The New People's Army (NPA), the armed wing of the CPP, was founded in March 1969. By the end of the Marcos era it was operating in 56 of the 73 provinces of the Philippines. According to Department of National Defense figures, by 1987 the CPP/NPA had more than 25,000 members, although this number is said to have declined in recent years. The National Democratic Front (NDF), a united front coalition controlled by the CPP, was established in 1973 and, like the CPP and NPA, it is outlawed by the government.

For much of its history the NPA has operated as a guerrilla army in rural areas. It has often relied on members of rural communities for the provision of food, shelter and logistical assistance. The NPA's close links with rural society, and the presence of NPA units in rural communities, have meant that inevitably ordinary people have been drawn into the conflict, at times unwillingly. Villagers who have refused to assist the NPA, or to join forces with them, have sometimes been dubbed opponents of the movement and have been subjected to human rights abuses. During the 1980s the NPA has also formed urban assassination squads, known as "sparrow units". The activities of these units have primarily consisted of the targeting and killing of suspected NPA opponents within the cities. Sparrow units have also reportedly been involved in acts of violence, such as the burning of buses, during general strikes.

The Moro National Liberation Front (MNLF), an armed organization advocating autonomy for the predominantly Muslim areas of Mindanao, was established in 1969 and emerged into the public arena in 1972.[9] It engaged the armed forces in full-scale conflict during the early 1970s, during which an estimated 50,000 to 60,000 people are believed to have died. The conflict subsided, although it did not end, with the signing of the Tripoli Agreement in December 1976. This provided for the eventual creation of an autonomous region consisting of 13 provinces. After 1977 there was little progress towards autonomy and at least three smaller armed opposition groups emerged to challenge the position of the MNLF: the Moro Islamic Liberation Front (MILF), the Bangsa Moro Liberation Front (BMLF) and the MNLF Reformist Group.[10] Talks between the new government and the MNLF in 1987 failed to produce an agreement on autonomy, but an "Organic Act of the Autonomous Region in Muslim Mindanao" was put to a plebiscite in November 1989. Nine of the 13 provinces in Mindanao rejected the Act, which was opposed by the MNLF. Sporadic fighting between government forces and the MNLF and among the various Muslim armed opposition groups has continued since then.

The Aquino Government

On 21 August 1983 Benigno Aquino, the husband of Corazon Aquino, was killed by military agents at Manila International Airport. He had just arrived back from the United States of America, where he had lived in exile after serving a prison sentence in the Philippines for his political activities. It was widely believed that President Marcos was responsible for the killing and this sparked massive demonstrations in Manila and elsewhere. The President was eventually forced to hold "snap" (unscheduled) presidential elections on 7 February 1986. These were contested by an opposition coalition led by Corazon Aquino. The elections took place amid widespread acts of violence and intimidation as well as allegations of fraud and electoral mismanagement. President Marcos initially claimed to have won the election, but the majority of the population were convinced that Corazon Aquino had won. On 16 February 1986 Aquino announced a campaign of non-violent civil disobedience, known as "People's Power", in protest at the outcome of the election.

Less than one week later, a group of rebel military officers headed by the Defense Secretary, Juan Ponce Enrile, retreated to the Armed Forces headquarters at Camp Aguinaldo to resist arrest for allegedly plotting a coup. Thousands of people flocked onto the EDSA highway,[11] preventing government troops from reaching the rebel forces. On 26 February 1986 Ferdinand Marcos and his family fled the country and Corazon Aquino was sworn in as President of the Philippines.

During the first months of the new government, President Aquino initiated negotiations to end the conflict between the armed forces and the NPA. A 60-day ceasefire agreement was reached between the National Democratic Front, negotiating on behalf of the NPA, and the armed forces. Peace talks were also set in motion but little progress was made. In January 1987 the NDF withdrew and the peace talks collapsed. The NDF did not return to the negotiations before the 60-day cease-fire expired and both sides gradually resumed fighting.

Between 1986 and late 1991 President Aquino's government faced six attempted military coups. Although none of the coup attempts succeeded in overthrowing the civilian government, the government increasingly conceded to the political demands of the military. Cabinet Ministers regarded as "leftists" by the Armed Forces of the Philippines were gradually removed from office; laws outlawing insurgent groups were maintained or reinforced; and the military was given almost complete autonomy in conducting the counter-insurgency campaign.

The 'Total Approach' to counter-insurgency

Following the collapse of peace negotiations in early 1987 the government introduced a campaign referred to as the "total approach"[12] to counter-insurgency. Its objective was to recover NPA-controlled areas and destroy the NPA's organizational and infrastructural base by 1992.[13] Aspects of the counter-insurgency strategy have contributed significantly to the pattern of extrajudicial executions, "disappearance" and other violations. The strategy has provided a political and military rationale for the commission of such violations and has created a climate in which they are highly likely to occur. In particular:

- it grants considerable operational autonomy to security force commanders at the regional and local level in the methods used to combat the insurgency;
- it has led to the organization of poorly disciplined militia forces and unofficial paramilitary groups whose existence the

government and military justifies in terms of national security;

- it has encouraged the practice of "red-labelling" critics or opponents of the government as "subversives" or CPP/NPA sympathizers.

The Philippine Senate Committee on Justice and Human Rights, which investigated the human rights situation in the country during 1989, drew similar conclusions. Its March 1990 report stated:

> *"The total approach strategy is considered a major factor contributing to the continuing human rights violations... Because of the total war policy, the accommodation of democratic dissent and respect for human rights is made more difficult".*

Similarly, the Philippine Government representative to the UN Commission on Human Rights in 1991 acknowledged that the counter-insurgency campaign was partly responsible for human rights violations. He stated:

> *"It is true that the armed conflict including the counter-insurgency policy pursued by the government to quell the resistance are factors contributing to the continuing human rights violations in the Philippines."*

Military authorities have both tacitly and explicitly condoned a policy which permits human rights violations, including the execution of unarmed civilians. One high-ranking military officer stated in 1988 that the counter-insurgency strategy involves the elimination of the NPA's mass base by "isolating" its "above-ground front organizations in the labour, student, urban poor, religious and other cause-oriented sectors". In practice, "isolation" has frequently meant the arbitrary arrest, "disappearance" or unlawful killing of suspected "communist" sympathizers. In 1990 a military officer said that this process of "isolation" was meant to show the population that "coddling" anti-government elements would "serve only to make their lives miserable".[14]

The government and the national military authorities generally claim that human rights violations that have occurred are isolated incidents, committed by military "scalawags" or "bad apples". Yet the considerable operational autonomy granted to field commanders permits such "isolated incidents" to occur on a wide scale. Under the current government, the AFP has replaced its 13 regional commands with six area commands each covering several provinces. Area commanders have been granted operational control over all troops within their region, enabling them to undertake operations without explicit permission or approval from general headquarters. Thus, while the national military command may determine broad lines of strategy, including measures for the protection of human rights, operational commanders are in practice often free to use extreme or unlawful measures.

Militia forces and paramilitaries

The counter-insurgency strategy has relied heavily on a network of about 90,000 members of official militia and semi-official paramilitary forces. These forces are in general poorly trained, poorly disciplined and possess only a rudimentary understanding of human rights. The existence of such a large and undisciplined force in itself inevitably increases the risk of human rights violations. In the Philippines the risk of abuse has been greatly increased through police and military authorities' apparent encouragement of such forces to act outside the law in the name of "national security".

Civilian militia forces have continued to play a key role in suppressing dissent or opposition in the Philippines despite various constitutional and legal provisions. The Civilian Home Defense Force (CHDF), which had been widely accused of responsibility for human rights violations under President Marcos, continued to function during 1989, despite the fact that President Aquino had issued an order for it to be dismantled in July 1987. Private armies and paramilitary forces, including the CHDF, are prohibited under Section 24 of Article XVIII of the 1987 Constitution (Transitory Provisions). However, the Constitution retains the idea of a "citizen armed force" in Article XVI. In accordance with this provision, the President issued Executive Order (EO) No. 264 in July 1987 establishing the Citizen Armed Force Geographical Unit (CAFGU). Senior military authorities argued that deployment of a militia force rather than a regular army against the armed opposition would be cost-effective under conditions of budgetary constraint.

The guidelines for the recruitment, training and mobilization of the CAFGU were intended to guarantee the formation of a well-disciplined auxiliary force operating under a clear chain of military command. In only a few years, however, the CAFGU gained a reputation for poor discipline and responsibility for widespread human rights violations. A substantial number of CAFGU members appear to have been recruited directly from the ranks of the discredited CHDF and a variety of unofficial vigilante groups. CAFGU members receive basic military training for periods of up to one month, but they appear to receive little if any education in basic principles of human rights. There is also evidence of forced recruitment into the CAFGU. Those who hesitate or refuse to join may be accused of sympathizing with the insurgency, and thereby placed at considerable personal risk.

In early 1987 the government also authorized the formation of Civilian Self Defense Organizations (CVOs), ostensibly neighbourhood groups set up to defend local communities. In October 1987 the government issued guidelines for the CVOs. These specified, among other things, that only CVO members permitted by law to bear arms, such as military and police reservists or private security guards, would be allowed to do so. In practice, the guidelines have often been disregarded and CVO members have been implicated in numerous human rights violations. Vigilante groups are also known to have operated under the guise of the CVO structure with the knowledge or support of military forces.

Despite the constitutional prohibition of unofficial armed groups, the military has used both CVOs and vigilante groups such as the *Alsa Masa* in the "counter-insurgency campaign. Government authorities and military officers have openly supported the creation of these groups while claiming that they have emerged "spontaneously". In March 1987 President Aquino publicly commended a vigilante group organized by the Governor of Davao del Sur. In April a presidential spokesman announced that the cabinet had achieved "unanimity of thought...endorsing voluntary and spontaneous [groups] of citizens for self-defence in areas where there was an insurgency". Soon afterwards, vigilante groups began to re-emerge throughout the country, organized and openly supported by local military, police or civilian officials.

Very soon there were numerous reports of grave human rights violations by members of CVO and vigilante groups. Pressure mounted for both to be disbanded. In July 1988 President Aquino told Congress that she had instructed the Chief of Staff to begin disbanding vigilante groups. However, two days later the Secretary of National Defense issued a "clarification", which stated that armed anti-communist civilian groups should not be disbanded

A member of a Citizen Armed Force Geographical Unit (CAFGU). CAFGUs replaced the Civilian Home Defense Force (CHDF), which was notorious for human rights abuses under President Marcos. CAFGUs quickly gained a similar reputation for poor discipline and widespread human rights violations. © Carol Lee

Members of Alsa Masa *vigilante group, Davao City, 1989. Unofficial armed groups such as* Alsa Masa *are prohibited by the Philippine Constitution. However, the authorities have openly supported the creation of such groups and the military has used them widely in its counter-insurgency campaign. Despite widespread reports of grave human rights violations committed by vigilante groups, and a 1988 presidential directive that such groups should be disbanded,* Alsa Masa *and other unofficial armed groups continue to operate alongside the military.*

because they were helping the fight against the communists. In March 1989 the Chief of the Philippine Constabulary reiterated this view when he told *Alsa Masa* members in Davao City that vigilante groups were an "effective military ally in the fight against communist insurgency". He said that they would not be disbanded on account of "unfounded criticism" of their human rights record. One year later the Senate Committee on Justice and Human Rights found that "many vigilante groups continue to exist and operate, despite the 1988 directive of President Aquino to disband them".

Amnesty International recognizes that the government has a right to counter threats to its security. It believes, however, that the government has an equal responsibility to ensure that any groups set up for this purpose, whether CAFGUs, CVOs or vigilantes, obey the law and do not violate human rights. Because of the deliberate incorporation of such groups in the government's counter-insurgency strategy, and the close cooperation between such groups and the regular armed forces, Amnesty International believes that the government must be held accountable for human rights violations committed by such groups.

The pattern of killing

Since 1986 the vast majority of extrajudicial executions in the Philippines have occurred in the context, or under the auspices, of counter-insurgency operations against the NPA and, to a lesser extent, the MNLF. For military purposes the counter-insurgency campaign has been divided into three phases, known as "clearing", "holding" and "consolidation".[15] Unlawful killings have occurred in all phases but the victims and the pattern have varied from one phase to the next.

The "clearing" phase involves full-scale combat operations, often including bombing and strafing from the air, by regular security forces in areas believed to be rebel strongholds. The objective of "clearing" operations is to destroy the NPA's military forces and remove the economic and social foundation of the rebel force. During this phase, people living in zones of conflict are at particular risk of extrajudicial execution because they are likely to be suspected of belonging to or sympathizing with guerrilla forces. Massacres of up to 20 people in a single village, including infants and the very elderly, have occurred when members of the security forces have taken revenge on local residents after members of the security forces have been killed. In some cases, civilians have been lined up and shot dead at close range. In others, people have been killed while sleeping or eating when their homes - generally constructed of light wood and bamboo - have been "strafed" without clear warning by soldiers using high-powered automatic weapons.

"Clearing" operations have caused the evacuation of about one million people in parts of Negros, Mindanao, Mindoro and northern Luzon since 1987.[16] People who have refused to leave their homes or who have attempted to return after temporary evacuation have often been accused of being rebels or rebel sympathizers; many of them have been threatened, ill-treated or extrajudicially executed by government and government-backed troops. Conditions in many of the evacuation centres have been poor and hundreds of people, many of them children, have died of disease.

The "holding" and "consolidation" phases of the counter-insurgency campaign involve efforts to weaken the organizational base of armed opposition groups. In practice, this has extended to weakening lawful civilian organizations and suppressing non-violent political opposition. The distinction between lawful non-violent opposition and armed opposition to the government has become blurred: critics of the government are likely to be regarded by the government or security forces as CPP/NPA supporters involved directly or indirectly in the armed insurgency.

In rural areas "holding" and "consolidation" operations rely heavily on CAFGUs, CVOs and vigilante groups working in cooperation with military Special Operation Teams (SOT). These operations attempt to identify and punish real or alleged rebel members and supporters within the local community. For example, people are often summoned to meetings, lectured on the evils of communism, then pressed to give the names of suspected communists. On the basis of such flimsy evidence - often entirely false - the people named are then subjected to harassment, arrest, "disappearance" or even extrajudicial execution.

The government has allowed "red-labelling" by military and police authorities to continue unchecked. Peasants, trade unionists, church, social and human rights activists have been accused by the authorities of being "communists", NPA members or members of CPP/NPA "front organizations" and portrayed as legitimate targets within the counter-insurgency campaign. Military or government officials have made such allegations in press and television interviews and at public meetings, ostensibly to alert the

Death threats against Sister Aquila Sy (above) were painted on the walls of a church (below) after she had been "red-labelled" a communist. Many church workers and members of lawful organizations, such as trade unions and human rights groups, have been publicly labelled by the military as "communist" and portrayed as legitimate targets within the counter-insurgency campaign. Once labelled, such people are likely to receive death threats from military sources or unofficial vigilante groups, and are at risk of "disappearing" or being killed.

community to the threat posed by the armed insurgency. Names have been placed on an "Order of Battle", a list of people wanted by the security forces for alleged subversion. In most cases the allegations are unproven and are denied by the organizations and individuals in question.

People who have been "red-labelled" live in fear for their lives: they know they may be killed or "disappear". They frequently receive death threats, either from military sources or from unofficial "vigilante" groups. Death threats are commonly made by telephone, over the radio, in personal letters, and in pamphlets and "hit lists" carrying the names of prospective targets of assassination. Military and police officers are known to have directly threatened political detainees, their relatives and their defence lawyers with death. Some officers have claimed this is a normal tactic of "psychological warfare" used against the "enemy". The evidence strongly suggests that people who have been publicly accused of "communist" sympathies or have received a death threat are much more likely to be killed.

3

The victims

The victims of political killings have come from all walks of life. They have included rural people living in zones of conflict, members of tribal communities, social and community workers, members of lawful political organizations, church workers, trade unionists and human rights lawyers.

The killings have taken place in a variety of circumstances. In rural areas people living in zones of suspected rebel activity have frequently died after their homes have been strafed with automatic weapons. Following these incidents the authorities have invariably claimed that the victims were killed during an armed encounter, but these claims have rarely been borne out by the evidence. In both rural and urban communities, those who have been "red-labelled" or threatened with death have been shot at home or in the street by small groups of armed men, who frequently attempt to conceal their identity. A significant number have been killed after being abducted or "disappeared" by members of the security forces. The bodies of these victims have been found days or weeks later, often in isolated locations and sometimes bearing signs of torture. In a few cases the authorities have acknowledged that an individual died in military or police custody but have claimed that he or she committed suicide or was killed while attempting to escape. In these cases, however, forensic evidence has indicated that the victims were tortured before being killed, or bound at the time of death, thus raising questions about the truth of official accounts.

This chapter gives information about the deaths of 85 people believed to have been victims of extrajudicial execution between 1988 and 1991. The cases are typical of scores of others. Taken together they give a picture of extrajudicial execution in the Philippines and provide evidence of a pattern of government, military and police responsibility for the political killings.

In the cases that follow only one of those believed to have committed the killings has been brought to justice. Amnesty International has written to the government to request information about official investigations into these killings and has explicitly sought information or the arrest, prosecution and conviction of those believed responsible. Government and military authorities have persistently failed to provide substantive replies to these requests.[17]

Some of the deaths have been officially investigated and information about such investigations has been included where available. In many instances those identified as the killers are believed to be still at large. Some remain as active members of military or militia units. This increases the distress and anxiety felt by relatives of the victims and decreases the likelihood of witnesses coming forward to testify before the courts or other investigative agencies. Amnesty International urges the government to renew the investigations into these and all extrajudicial killings and to ensure that the perpetrators are suspended from active service and brought to justice.

Rural dwellers in areas of armed conflict

Rural dwellers have figured prominently among those killed by government or government-backed forces in recent years. Many have been killed after military or paramilitary units using automatic weapons strafed their bamboo homes or the fields where they were working. Villagers have also been "invited for questioning" and taken to unoccupied buildings or huts before being stabbed or shot. Their bodies have been dumped by the roadside or in rivers and many have been found mutilated or with signs of torture. Sometimes the bodies have been burned, along with the buildings in which the victims were killed. On occasions, entire families have been shot dead apparently in "revenge" for the death of a member of military or paramilitary forces during an armed encounter.

The military has consistently claimed that the victims, who have included many elderly people, women and children, were NPA members killed in the course of armed combat. The incidents described below, however, suggest that the deliberate and arbitrary killing of unarmed civilians is widespread in rural areas. In all the case studies, available information indicates that the victims were unarmed and defenceless at the time of death. Moreover, they were not killed during armed encounters, and most had no apparent connection with the armed opposition.

Renante Morales and Dante Morales: 3 June 1988, Leyte

Renante Morales, aged 14, and his 16-year-old brother, Dante Morales, were detained and killed on 3 June 1988 while working in the family field in *barangay* Monterico, Baybay, Leyte. Their father, Feliciano Morales and eight-year-old Feliciano Jr saw the killings and identified the perpetrators as members of the 43rd Infantry Battalion (IB) of the Philippine Army (PA) along with members of a vigilante group.

According to Feliciano Morales, he and his sons heard gunshots when they were harvesting and realised they were surrounded by a group of soldiers. Feliciano Morales climbed onto a large rock and waved his arms shouting at the armed men to stop shooting because his family might be hit. The shooting continued. His sons ran to hide in the tall grass, but the soldiers found Dante and Renante Morales and took them to the middle of the field. One of the soldiers reportedly suggested that they should kill them so the NPA could be blamed for their deaths. From his hiding place, Feliciano Morales saw two of the vigilantes, whom he knew, hack Dante Morales with a *bolo* (machete) until he was dead. Renante Morales was then made to kneel and was shot from behind. His body was dumped in a nearby stream.

Feliciano Jr was detained by the soldiers after they found him hiding nearby. Amnesty International was subsequently informed that he had been adopted by a military officer who resisted efforts by the Morales family to have him returned. The CHR and the Senate Committee on Justice and Human Rights were informed of this "adoption" but knowledge of it was denied by the military on 20 November 1989. To Amnesty International's knowledge criminal charges have not been brought against the suspected killers; nor have they been the subject of any disciplinary action whatsoever.

Jaime Vaflor and Rogelio Vaflor, and Felipe Gantalao: 16 September 1988, Zamboanga del Sur

Three residents of *barangay* San Antonio, Tukuran, Zamboanga del Sur, were tortured and executed on 16 September 1988 while in the custody of members of the Scout Rangers of the PA. Eyewitnesses testified in sworn affidavits that Rogelio Vaflor, aged 26, and his brother, Jaime, aged 21, were arrested by soldiers earlier that day after a civilian, whose identity was concealed by the military, had identified them as NPA members. They were taken to an isolated area of the *barangay*. Their hands were tied and they were beaten for five hours as the soldiers tried to force them to admit they were NPA members. They were then shot dead with automatic weapons.

An eye-witness testified that a relative of the victims, Felipe Gantalao, aged 49, ran towards the Vaflor's house after hearing the gunfire. He was stopped by the Scout Rangers and taken to the bodies of the victims. He was then tortured and shot.

An autopsy report confirmed that all three had been severely tortured and that Jaime Vaflor had been castrated. Seventeen members of the armed forces were arrested in connection with the killings, but all were acquitted by a military court in December 1990. Details of any further official investigation have not been made public by the authorities and Amnesty International is not aware of any disciplinary measures against the military suspects.

The Pagao Family: 18 February 1989, Western Samar

Pedro and Encarnacion Pagao and their two children, nine-year-old Eduardo and six-year-old Rosalia, were shot dead on 18 February 1989, reportedly by troops of the 62nd IB in *sitio* Bangon, *barangay* Carayman, Calbayog City, Samar. Four unidentified people were killed at the same time. A relative of the victims reported that a Major from the 62nd IB admitted that his battalion had killed the Pagao family. The military claimed the eight were NPA rebels killed during an armed encounter with government soldiers.

The military prevented relatives from retrieving the bodies. In March 1989 an exhumation and fact-finding team, which included representatives from the National Bureau of Investigation (NBI) and the CHR, was also prevented by the military from reaching the site of the killings. A second investigation team reached the site in August 1989 and found remains of at least four of the victims, including the two children, in shallow graves.

The CHR's report said that there was "no doubt" that elements of the 62nd IB were responsible for the killings. It disputed the military claim that the victims were NPA rebels, saying that evidence indicated that the Pagaos were civilians. It concluded that the incident: "was not an encounter but rather a strafing and massacre committed by military soldiers..." The CHR report made recommendations for further investigations to identify the perpetrators "so that proper charges may be brought against them". However, none of the suspects has been arrested and no formal inquest was conducted by the military authorities.

By November 1991 one of the suspected killers had reportedly been killed and the whereabouts of three others remained unknown. No progress on the investigation had been made public. The CHR had promised to pay the relatives 40,000 pesos in compensation, but by mid-1991 no compensation was believed to have been received.[18]

Teodoro Egoc Sr, Jimmy Estoque, Nicasio, Hernani and Reggie Opiar: 29 March 1989, Negros Oriental

Teodoro Egoc Sr, Jimmy Estoque, Nicasio Opiar and his two children, four-year-old Hernani and two-year old Reggie, were killed on 29 March 1989 in *sitio* Kabatangbatangan, *barangay* Buenavista, Sta. Catalina, Negros Oriental. The victims, along with one other, were arrested and taken away while working on their land. Other members of their families were present and identified the perpetrators as members of the local CAFGU, vigilantes and two unidentified PC officials. One of those arrested managed to escape with gunshot wounds in his back and he testified that the others had been mutilated and killed.

The bodies were found on 1 April 1989 in an abandoned house known to be used by the alleged perpetrators as a meeting place. Relatives believed the killers had accused the adult victims of being NPA sympathizers because they had refused to join the CAFGU.

The *Manila Chronicle* of 27 September reported that the PC commander had denied military involvement in the incident and stated that allegations against the security forces were "just another lie and malicious concoction of the enemies of the state in order to disparage the military". Nevertheless, in May 1989 the CHR and the Department of Justice affirmed that they had investigated the case and that charges would be filed against the suspects in July 1989. Amnesty International wrote to the CHR in May 1991 and requested information on the prosecution of those suspected to have killed the five people. The CHR provided no information indicating that the suspects had indeed been charged or otherwise brought to justice.

The Paombong Killings: 28 April 1989, Bulacan

On 28 April 1989 nine fishpond workers, including a man in his seventies and a 13-year-old girl, were reportedly killed by soldiers from the 42nd Marine Battalion in *barangay* San Jose, Paombong, Bulacan. Military officials initially claimed they had killed nine NPA members. However, when relatives and the fishpond owner insisted the victims were simply working at the fishpond, the military revised their story and said the victims were civilians caught in cross-fire between the Marines and NPA forces. They further claimed that the nine had sheltered NPA members who had then killed them.

Information gathered by human rights groups indicated that none of the fishpond workers had any links with the NPA. They concluded that an armed encounter between NPA forces and the Marines may have taken place *prior* to the killings, resulting in the death of one Marine, and that the murder of the nine was an act of revenge by Marines who returned to the fishpond after the encounter. This version of events was consistent with the initial findings of a local municipal health officer who conducted an autopsy on the victims soon after their deaths. The autopsy revealed that three of the victims had died before the others, and that they were all apparently shot dead from close range while lying on the ground.

The autopsy also revealed that some of the victims may have been tortured. It stated that the head of a 70-year-old man had been bludgeoned with a shovel. A 13-year-old girl had cuts on both wrists, a mangled shoulder, a nearly severed neck and facial burns. Others had burns on their bodies. One man reportedly had a gash on his face; one of his sons had fractured bones, arms and legs twisted out of shape and his fingers almost severed from his hand.

In June 1989 an investigation team, which included NBI representatives, concluded that an armed encounter between the 42nd Marine Battalion and the NPA had occurred, during which the nine had been killed. It exonerated the Marines believed to have been involved in the incident. A presidential investigation committee also concluded that the nine were killed in an armed encounter.

The CHR published its own report in August 1990. It also concluded that the victims had died during an armed encounter. Despite the existence of substantial forensic evidence, it noted only that "the nature of the injuries found on the victims indicates they *could* have been tortured..." (emphasis added). The evidence of torture cast serious doubt on claims that they had been killed in crossfire. Nevertheless, the CHR absolved the military suspects of responsibility and, without providing any supporting evidence, suggested that the NPA forces "had more opportunity" to inflict torture on the victims. One of the CHR commissioners dissented from this view and questioned whether there had actually been an encounter.Military authorities are believed to have provided some financial compensation to the victims' relatives, but there have been no arrests in connection with the massacre and no one has been brought before a court. It was reported in 1991 that the alleged perpetrators were still on "inactive service". Amnesty International wrote to President Aquino on 12 May 1989 and provided details of reports of the torture and killing of the nine fishpond workers. No substantive reply was received to that letter, nor to further requests for information sent to the government in May 1991.

Guarina Celso and Raquel Gorpido:
13 July 1989, Northern Samar

On 13 July 1989 two women, Guarina Celso and Raquel Gorpido, and one man, were arrested by a group of 50 men identified as soldiers from the 19th IB and members of a local CAFGU in *sitio* Batac, Mondragon, Northern Samar. They were arrested after a CAFGU member had accused the women of being NPA members.

The arrested man escaped from his assailants on 14 July. In a sworn affidavit he testified that the women were taken to a house, where their hands were tied behind their backs and they were kicked and hit by the soldiers. Later the trousers of both women were cut into pieces. The pieces were put into the women's mouths. The commanding captain slashed and stabbed the women's ears with a hunting knife. Guarina Celso was raped by the captain and both women were raped by more than half the group of CAFGU members and soldiers.

According to the witness, the military and CAFGU members took the women the following day to a place near a river in *barangay* Flormina, Mondragon. The commanding captain sliced off the pudenda of the women with his hunting knife and stabbed Guarina Celso to death. A CAFGU member stabbed Raquel Gorpido to death. They were then buried nearby.

Relatives of the victims were afraid to recover the bodies after they received word that it would be dangerous for them to do so. On 16 August 1989 a fact-finding team headed by the Samar office of the CHR found freshly dug soil and uncovered 25 small pieces of human bone and an abaca rope. It was feared that the bodies may have been removed after an account of the murders appeared in the *Philippine Daily Globe* on 4 August 1989.

In August 1989 relatives filed a complaint with the provincial prosecutor against the suspected perpetrators, including the commanding captain, members of his command and one CAFGU member. The regional CHR office in Samar recommended to the prosecutor that charges be filed and the accused suspended or dismissed from the armed forces. After these proceedings had been set in motion, the eye-witness and relatives of the murdered women again reportedly received threats from those believed responsible. On local radio stations the military claimed that the eye-witness was an NPA member. At a hearing conducted by the CHR in October, a military colonel from Samar claimed that the allegations against the military were false. He said the women had been released from custody before being raped and killed. The CHR chairman accepted this denial without question, despite the eye-witness account and forensic evidence which supported allegations of military involvement in the torture and killings. The CHR chairman declared that the regional CHR office in Samar had "fabricated" the case and accused the eye-witness of false testimony. The case of the two women was "archived", the witness withdrew his complaint and the CHR officer in Samar was transferred.

To Amnesty International's knowledge no further action has been taken on this case and no arrests have been made. The military captain believed responsible for the unit which carried out these unlawful acts has not been the subject of any disciplinary proceedings. One or more of the alleged perpetrators are reported to have been transferred to another region.

Rommel Muscosa: 19 August 1989, Eastern Samar

Four-year-old Rommel Muscosa was killed on 19 August 1989 when members of the 34th IB and a local CAFGU fired automatic weapons into his family's house in *barangay* San Andres, Borongan, Eastern Samar. His brothers - Charlie, aged 10, and Ferdinand, aged six, witnessed the killing. They said that a soldier entered the house after the strafing and fired another shot at Rommel who was lying wounded on the floor. Rommel sustained gunshot wounds to the head, abdomen and legs. Ferdinand was wounded, but Charlie was not harmed. The military claimed that three NPA members had been seen in the house earlier that day. Eye-witnesses confirmed this claim but said that soldiers had already seen the NPA members leaving the house before they began shooting.

Witnesses identified the perpetrators but relatives were too afraid to file charges and opted for an amicable settlement. They have reportedly received some financial compensation from the military. In January 1990 a warrant for the arrest of one of the suspects was issued for his alleged involvement in the murder of another resident of the village, Edito Barcel, on 5 October 1989. However, despite evidence of the suspect's involvement in two murders, the warrant for his arrest was reportedly not served by the police authorities. In July 1991 the suspect was still believed to be an active CAFGU member based at Camp Asidillo in Borongan.

Emelyn Lipon: 28 June 1990, Bukidnon

Nine-year old Emelyn Lipon was killed and four others were wounded on 28 June 1990 when several armed men believed to be CAFGU members strafed a house in *barangay* Lumbo, Valencia, Bukidnon. Eye-witnesses said that one hour after the incident, a CAFGU member returned and put a weapon beside one of the victims. Minutes later another CAFGU member returned and accused the wounded of being NPA members.

A warrant of arrest for the CAFGU members was issued by the Valencia Municipal Trial Court judge on 13 July 1990 but no arrests were made. In October and November 1990 the Justice Department, the Department of National Defense and PC national headquarters instructed the local police to serve the warrant on the grounds that complainants and witnesses may have been in danger while the suspects were at large. Police authorities provided verbal assurances that action would be taken, but failed to serve the warrant. To Amnesty International's knowledge the suspected CAFGU members had not been arrested by November 1991.

Kamlon Mamindiala and family: 3 August 1990, Sultan Kudarat

On 3 August 1990, 19 members of a Muslim family, including a pregnant woman and six children, were killed by soldiers of the 38th IB in *barangay* New Passi, Tacurong, Sultan Kudarat. The military initially claimed that all were victims of an armed encounter between soldiers and Muslim rebels. However, a report by the PC/INP provincial commander, dated August 1990, confirmed allegations that the victims were in fact extrajudicially executed by soldiers.

According to eye-witnesses, the soldiers went to the home of Kamlon Mamindiala to arrest him as a suspected Muslim rebel. Kamlon Mamindiala was reported to have killed two of the soldiers while resisting arrest. The remaining soldiers killed him as he tried to escape. The soldiers then ordered his relatives, including those from two nearby houses, to stand outside their homes where they were shot dead. The victims included Kamlon Mamindiala's parents, his pregnant wife and their six children aged between one and 13 years.

The Secretary of National Defense ordered an investigation into the killings and this resulted in the temporary suspension from duty of the 38th IB commander and the suspension of two other officers and 12 soldiers. A military court acquitted all the suspects in March 1991 and the men were reportedly returned to active service with the 38th IB sometime during the year.

Amnesty International wrote to President Aquino and the Secretary of National Defense in September 1990. The letters expressed concern at the killings, welcomed the proposed investigation and asked to be kept informed of its progress. No substantive reply was received to these letters. Amnesty International wrote again to the Secretary of National Defense and the CHR in May 1991, expressing regret that the court proceedings had not resulted in convictions of those found guilty of killing Kamlon Mamindiala and his family. The CHR expressed its regret in a subsequent letter to Amnesty International, but provided no indication that it would pursue its investigations into this case.[19] To Amnesty International 's knowledge, by November 1991 there had been no further efforts by the authorities to ensure that those responsible for the killings were brought to justice.

The Peralta Family: 16 August 1990, Pangasinan

On 16 August 1990 a father and his three sons were killed by armed men believed to be acting unofficially under orders from a local police sergeant. Domingo Peralta and two of his sons, Manny, aged 16, and Noel, aged 20, were shot dead inside their home in *barangay* Manlocboc, Aquilar, Pangasinan. Neighbours heard three single shots and successive bursts of gunfire. A nine-year-old son, Ricky, who was playing outside the house, was shot and wounded. He was then dragged inside the house where the bodies of his father and brothers lay. According to reports the armed men set fire to the house, which burned down with the wounded boy and his dead relatives inside it.

Neighbours believed that the killings had taken place because the sergeant had accused another of Domingo Peralta's sons of being an NPA member. It was also revealed that Domingo Peralta had been aware of the INP sergeant's involvement in *jueteng* (illegal gambling). Following the killings the remaining family members left the area for fear of further violence. However, after the incident was reported to national human rights organizations, armed men were reported to have gone to the town where the Peralta family had taken refuge and searched for them there.

The Department of Justice, the NBI and the CHR conducted investigations into the case. These were apparently hampered by the reluctance of witnesses to come forward and testify for fear of reprisals. By mid-1991 the Provincial Prosecutor's office in Pangasinan had filed criminal charges against a PNP sergeant and two other PNP members in connection with the murders. The Prosecutor found sufficient evidence for the three to be brought to trial. He recommended the filing of charges for multiple murder and arson. A warrant of arrest with no bail recommended was issued against the three. The sergeant suspected of carrying out the killings was placed under "technical arrest" but was reportedly seen frequently in the vicinity of the killings during the early part of 1991. The other suspects are believed to remain at large.

Nory Aballa, Leonardo Plohimon: 2 March 1991, Negros Occidental

The charred bodies of Nory Aballa and Leonardo Plohimon, both farmers, were found two days after they were abducted by military officials on 2 March 1991 in *barangay* Locotan, Kabankalan, Negros Occidental. Nory Aballa's brother reported that at about 5am on 2 March, the household was awakened by military men from the 66th IB of the PA based in Kabankalan town. The military demanded chicken and eggs, which the family provided. Nory Aballa and Leonardo Plohimon were then reportedly seized and taken to the military detachment, apparently without any explanation.

Later in the day Nory Aballa's mother went with the wife of Leonardo Plohimon to the military detachment in Kabankalan to press for the release of the two. The women reported being made to sign a paper stating that Nory Aballa and Leonardo Plohimon had been released in good condition. However, military officials said that in fact the two would not be released until the following day. Military officials said the two men were to be used as "guides" in the neighbourhood.

On 4 March family members found the burned bodies of Nory Aballa and Leonardo Plohimon which had been dumped nearby. Marks on the bodies indicated the victims had been stabbed and shot before they were burned along with the hut in which they had been held. Amnesty International is not aware of any official investigation into the abduction and death of Nory Aballa and Leonardo Plohimon.

Helen Salita: 4 June 1991, Surigao del Norte

A mother of seven, 44-year-old Helen Salita was shot dead while holding her baby at her home in *barangay* Pautao, Bacuag, Surigao del Norte. The killing was believed to have been carried out by a CAFGU member based in the *barangay*.

One of the victim's daughters reported to a local human rights organization that the incident occurred at about 7pm on 4 June 1991. She said that Helen Salita was standing at the window and cuddling her baby when two gunshots were heard. Her son, aged eight, said he had seen a man in military uniform about two metres from the house moments before the killing. He said the man was sitting down and aiming a rifle at the room where his mother was. This statement was borne out when, the following day, traces of combat boot-prints were found at the back of the house.

Following the shooting a CAFGU member, who had been a friend of Helen Salita, attended the wake and reportedly identified a CAFGU member from *barangay* Pautao as the killer. He also identified an empty rifle shell which had been found near the house after the shooting. However, a CAFGU member from *barangay* Pautao subsequently visited Helen Salita's husband, Osias, and reportedly threatened that he might be the next to be killed. The Salitas' daughter said that CAFGU members had interrogated Osias Salita before and had attempted to discover the whereabouts of her two brothers, who had allegedly joined the NPA. Because of continuing threats the Salita family left their home.

To Amnesty International's knowledge the government had not initiated an official investigation into the death of Helen Salita; nor had the suspected murderer been disciplined or brought to justice by the end of November 1991.

Members of tribal communities

Members of tribal communities have frequently been the victims of serious human rights violations, as have those working for and with them. The term "tribal peoples" is commonly used in the Philippines to describe the many non-Muslim, ethno-linguistic groups who generally live in isolated upland areas. The largest groupings of tribal peoples are the Igorot of the Cordillera mountains of northern Luzon and the Lumad of Mindanao. They number about one million and two million respectively.

Members of tribal communities have been the victims of human rights violations primarily because of the political and economic significance of the land which they inhabit. Upland areas of Luzon and Mindanao in particular have for years been important base areas for the two major armed opposition groups, the NPA and — in Mindanao — the MNLF. The government effort to defeat these rebel groups has entailed full-scale military operations in areas of suspected rebel activity. This has resulted in a number of deaths of unarmed civilians including tribal peoples.

The lands inhabited by many tribal communities are also of considerable economic value. Resistance to the exploitation of the land and its natural resources has placed many communities in conflict with powerful commercial interests and not infrequently with the government's own security forces. Organizations established to defend tribal community interests have often been labelled by the military as fronts for the CPP/NPA and leaders or members of such organizations have become the victims of extra-judicial execution and other violations.

Robert Estimada and Ferdinand Bragas: 22 July 1988, Mountain Province

In the early morning of 22 July 1988, Robert Estimada and Ferdinand Bragas, were killed in Bontoc, Mountain Province, in circumstances which strongly suggested military, police or paramilitary involvement. The two victims were both staff members of the Development Agency for the Tribes of the Cordillera (DATC): Robert Estimada had been an artist and cartographer and Ferdinand Bragas a community organizer.

On the evening of 21 July, the 192nd PC Company was reportedly on red alert in Bontoc town, Mountain Province. Soldiers were deployed in the area. That evening Robert Estimada and Ferdinand Bragas went to a "folkhouse" (a bar with folk singers), where they

Robert Estimada (above) and Ferdinand Bragas (below) were killed in July 1988 after being shot at close range and stabbed with ice picks. Both were activists with a group promoting tribal rights in the Cordillera region, Northern Luzon, which had been labelled by the military as "communist". Shortly before their deaths they were seen in the presence of two policemen.

were apparently joined by two policemen and two women. Robert Estimada and Ferdinand Bragas left the bar at around 1am. Shortly afterwards they were shot at close range and stabbed with ice picks near a bridge. Residents of nearby houses reported being too frightened to approach the wounded men. After about 30 minutes a vehicle was said to have arrived and to have taken them to hospital. Ferdinand Bragas was dead on arrival and Robert Estimada died two hours later.

The following day, 22 July, a folk-singer and correspondent for a local paper was summoned to the Bontoc Police Station. He was interviewed and then issued a press release which stated that rivalry over women was the motive for the killing of Robert Estimada and Ferdinand Bragas.However, local residents and members of the DATC believed that the killings were probably connected to the victims' activities with the DATC, an organization which had frequently been labelled by the military as "communist".

The perpetrators of the killings have never been identified. However, circumstantial evidence indicated that members of the PC and a paramilitary group may have been responsible. A military informer had reportedly told a staff member of the

DATC that Robert Estimada and Ferdinand Bragas had been under surveillance since June 1988. The night before their deaths they were seen with police and military men, as well as members of a paramilitary group known as the Municipal Security Unit (MSU), which had recently been set up by the Mayor of Bontoc. Residents also observed that it had taken an unusually long time for the police to take the victims to the hospital. Finally, local people believed that without military or police complicity, a murderer would have had difficulty escaping from the scene of a crime which took place during a military operation.

Although there have been official investigations by the PC/INP and the CHR, to Amnesty International's knowledge no arrests have been made and there have been no court proceedings. Relatives have not received compensation nor have they filed a case against the military suspects, apparently because of fears for their safety.

Ayangwa Claver was killed in January 1990 by a single gun shot fired at close range into the back of his neck. Witnesses claimed that at least two of his killers were linked with a military intelligence group operating in the area. There was widespread speculation that his killing was meant to intimidate his father, a Congressman and leading advocate of tribal people's rights in the Cordillera, Northern Luzon.

Ayangwa Claver, Oliver Castro and Pedro Bulayao: 21 January 1990, Kalinga-Apayao

Ayangwa Claver, Oliver Castro and Pedro Bulayao were shot dead by a group of heavily armed men in the town of Pinukpuk, Kalinga-Apayao on 21 January 1990. Ayangwa Claver reportedly died of a single gun shot fired at close range in the back of the neck. Eye-witnesses said the perpetrators wore civilian clothing and claimed that at least two were linked with a military intelligence group operating in the province.

Ayangwa Claver was the son of Congressman William Claver, well known for his advocacy of tribal people's rights. Congressman Claver served as Chairman of the Cordillera People's Alliance (CPA) and was active in the movement for regional autonomy in the Cordillera. The killing of the three named above took place less than two weeks before the holding of a plebiscite on the Cordillera Organic Act, a government-sponsored plan for autonomy which the CPA had opposed and which was rejected in all but one province. Congressman Claver had previously been accused by local military authorities of having NPA sympathies and had reportedly received death threats. There was speculation that the killing of Ayangwa Claver and his friends was intended to silence or intimidate Congressman Claver.

Peasant activists and farmers' union members

A significant number of peasant organizers and members of farmers' unions have been victims of extrajudicial killings. Peasants and farmers from the Visayas region in the central Philippines appear to have been the most frequently targeted by government and government-backed forces. In 1991 Amnesty International recorded the deaths of at least five farmers' union members on Samar alone. The majority of the victims were actively involved in developmental projects for farmers or in lobbying the authorities for a more equitable distribution of land.

Juanito Lobaton: 31 July 1989, Negros Occidental

The body of 50-year-old Juanito Lobaton, married with 10 children and a member of a sugar growers' association, was found in a shallow grave two days after he had been arrested by CAFGU members on 31 July 1989.

Five armed, uniformed CAFGU members reportedly approached Juanito Lobaton and his son, Jerry, when they were delivering a cartload of wood. Jerry Lobaton identified one of the CAFGU members by name and reported that he was stationed at the 601st PA detachment in *barangay* Marcelo, Calatrava, Negros Occidental. The CAFGU members interrogated Juanito Lobaton about the NPA and told him he was a suspected NPA sympathizer. The CAFGU member ordered Jerry Lobaton to go home, threatening to kill him if he refused, and took Juanito Lobaton to their detachment.

The following day relatives tried to locate Juanito Lobaton but CAFGU members denied the arrest. On 2 August the mutilated body of Juanito Lobaton was found by small children at *barangay* Minapasok, Calatrava. The victim had been gashed in the neck and his breast and armpits stabbed. His elbows and knees were broken, some of his teeth had been wrenched out of the mouth, and his hands were tied with a piece of rope.

In July 1991, two years after the killing took place, it was reported that relatives were too afraid to file a complaint with the courts or the CHR because the suspected perpetrators were still at large. The government is believed to have taken no steps to initiate an independent inquiry into this apparent extrajudicial execution or to provide adequate protection to the relatives of Juanito Lobaton.

Diomedes Abawag and Nestor Loberio: 29 January 1990, Samar

Diomedes Abawag and Nestor Loberio, a staff worker and project director at Samar Assistance for Farmers Development Inc.

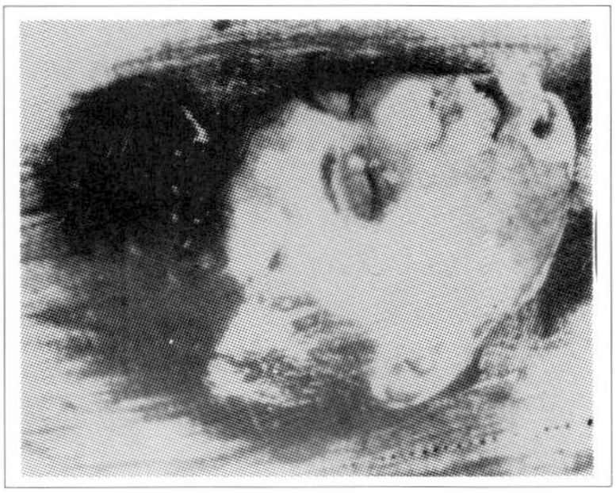

Diomedes Abawag (above) was tortured and beheaded after being abducted in January 1990 by armed men believed to be members of a vigilante group backed by a military intelligence unit. His mutilated head was later found in the sea by fishermen. Nestor Loberio (below) was abducted at the same time and has since "disappeared". Both men worked for a farming development project in Samar, whose staff had received threats from members of the security forces.

(SAFDI), were abducted by armed men on 29 January 1990 in Catbalogan, Samar. The unidentified perpetrators, who were driving a military vehicle, were believed to be members of a vigilante group set up by a military intelligence unit based at Camp Lukban in Catbalogan.

Diomedes Abawag was apparently tortured and beheaded by his captors. His head was found in the sea by fishermen near *barangay* Butaena, Zumarraga, Samar on 1 February 1990. It bore signs of torture, including a deep slash in the lower lip, facial bruises and a hole in the right temple, The whereabouts of Nestor Loberio remain unknown.[20]

An NBI investigation into the killings of Diomedes Abawag and Nestor Loberio revealed that the offices of SAFDI, a lawful non-governmental organization involved in development projects for farmers in Samar, had been visited several times by members of the security forces. SAFDI staff were also reported to have been threatened. Military and police authorities were reported to have suspected SAFDI members of engaging in fundraising for the NPA.

Amnesty International has submitted information about the deaths of Nestor Loberio and Diomedes Abawag to the government on at least two occasions, but has received nor reply to its communications. The progress and outcome of investigations reportedly conducted by the NBI and the CHR have not been made public and to Amnesty International's knowledge there have been no arrests in connection with these killings.

Diosdado Evasco, Nerry Dulay: 7 February 1991, Northern Samar

Diosdado Evasco and Nerry Dulay were killed by armed men identified by eye-witnesses as members of the 19th IB of the PA and a local CAFGU unit. On 7 February 1991 the two visited the home of the captain of *barangay* Lao-angan, San Roque, Northern Samar. During the visit troops reportedly strafed the house, killing Diosdado Evasco and Nerry Dulay. At least three others were wounded. They included Diosdado Evasco's wife and another woman — both of whom were pregnant — and his 18-year-old son.

Prior to the killings an officer from the 19th IB had reportedly accused the group TIPANAN, a church-based socio-economic project in the area, of being a communist front organization. In response to these allegations, the Municipal Peace and Order Council in San Roque had convened a meeting and, in the presence of the 19th IB officer, members of TIPANAN protested against the allegations. It is not clear whether Diosdado Evasco and Nerry Dulay attended that meeting, but residents in San Roque believe that their deaths were a consequence of these events.

According to reports the alleged perpetrators surrendered, but no disciplinary action has been taken against them. An official investigation was conducted by both military and police authorities, but the results have not been made public. To Amnesty International's knowledge, no case has yet been brought before the courts.

Renato Tabasa Zabate: 8 September 1991, Cebu

Renato Tabasa Zabate, a 21-year-old member of the United Farmers' Organization (UFO), was found dead on 13 September 1991, five days after being abducted by unidentified armed men, thought to be linked to the PNP, in Canduman, Mandaue City, Cebu. His body bore clear signs of torture.

According to reports, Renato Tabasa Zabate left the house of relatives with a friend at about 1pm on 8 September. As the two walked down the road they noticed several armed men drinking beer in the street. Two of the men approached them and held guns to the backs of Renato and his friend. Renato Tabasa Zabate was then reportedly pushed into a waiting jeep and driven away in the direction of Talamban. Information from unofficial sources indicated that Renato Tabasa Zabate may have been taken to the Cebu Metropolitan District Command Headquarters of the PNP at Camp Sotero in Cebu City.

The body of Renato Tabasa Zabate was found on 13 September by schoolchildren in Sogod, some 62 kilometres north of Cebu City. The victim had been tied with electrical wire and gagged with his own towel. An autopsy revealed 31 abrasions, contusions and wounds on different parts of the body. Strangulation was stated to have been the probable cause of death.

It is believed that the death of Renato Tabasa Zabate may have been linked to his activities with UFO, an organization which is affiliated to a militant peasant organization in Cebu province. During the early part of 1990 members of UFO and other workers' organizations in the region were reportedly harassed and intimidated by military forces and anti-communist vigilante groups for being suspected NPA supporters. Renato Tabasa Zabate's wife, whose relatives are also active in UFO, faces charges of subversion along with four others in Cebu City.[21] In May 1987 Renato Tabasa Zabate was arrested and detained by military agents. He was held

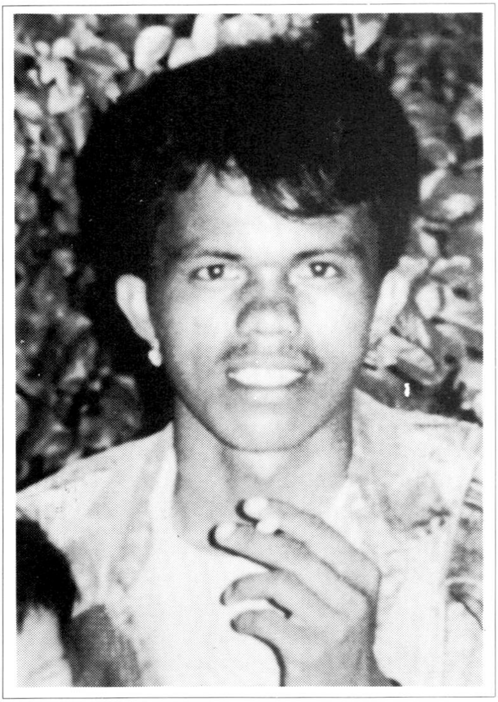

Renato Tabasa Zabate (left) was an organizer for the United Farmers' Organization, whose members had frequently been harassed by the military and anti-communist vigilante groups. He was abducted by armed men in September 1991. Five days later his body was found by schoolchildren, bound with electrical wire and gagged with a towel (below). An autopsy found 31 wounds on the body.

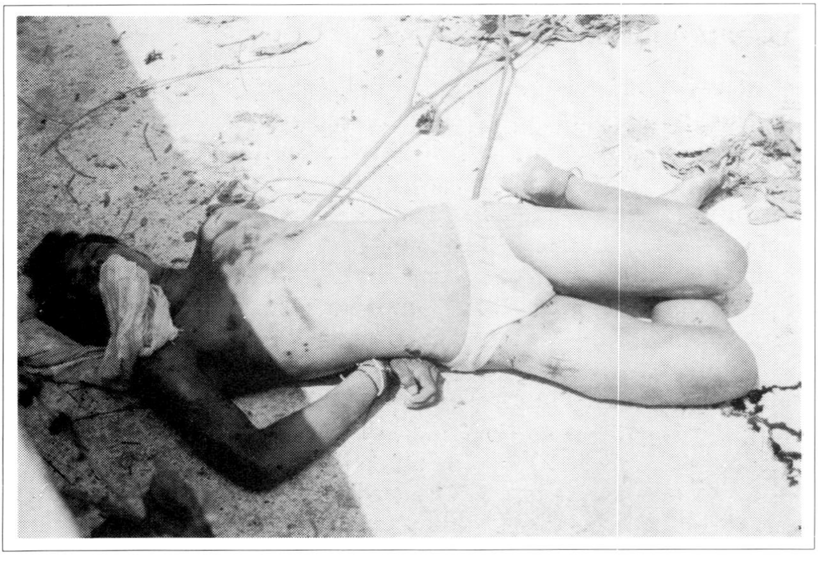

in custody at a "safehouse" (an unofficial detention centre) to the southwest of Cebu City along with two others. The three were released 11 hours later without charge.

To Amnesty International's knowledge, no official investigation into the death of Renato Tabasa Zabate had been initiated by November 1991.

Leonilo Sabarita: 3 November 1991, Davao City

Leonilo Sabarita, President of the Farmers' Association in Davao City (FADC) was shot dead on 3 November 1991 by unidentified armed men at his home in *sitio* Cawa-cawa, Mintal, Davao City. According to the victim's mother, he was gunned down at around 8pm. Eye-witnesses to the killing took Leonilo Sabarita to the Davao Medical Centre but he was dead on arrival. Leonilo Sabarita was 30 years old and father of five children.

FADC members believed that the killing may have been politically motivated. They said that Leonilo Sabarita had been accused by the vigilante group *Alsa Masa* of supporting the CPP/NPA. The FADC was also reportedly involved in organizing farmers' efforts to own their own land and to demilitarize zones in the region where they lived.

Amnesty International urges the government to initiate an immediate investigation into the death of Leonilo Sabarita and to ensure that those found responsible are brought promptly to justice.

Urban poor activists

In recent years the urban population of the Philippines has increased by approximately six per cent a year, largely because of rural migration to the cities. Lawful political organizations to assist the urban poor, including the expanding squatter communities, have emerged during the 1970s and 1980s. Urban organizations have organized resistance to forced evictions as well as campaigning to improve services such as garbage collection, water supply and drainage. Urban poor activists have also promoted development projects and workshops in the cities.

People involved in such activities have been accused by the military of involvement with the CPP/NPA and some have been killed by members of the security forces. In the following cases all the victims died in police custody, most after being arrested without apparent reason. The authorities claimed that the victims tried to escape or grab a weapon from their captors, or that they committed suicide. Forensic evidence available to the victims' lawyers and relatives has, however, called these claims into question.

Jacinto Mañaois: 20 October 1989, Manila

Jacinto Mañaois, a 33-year-old urban poor organizer, was arrested by police on 20 October 1989, ostensibly as a suspect in a car theft in Metro Manila. He was detained at the headquarters of the Northern Police District (NPD) in Quezon City. On 28 October his wife was informed that he had been shot while in the custody of three policemen, allegedly after he had tried to grab a gun.

These claims were contested by Jacinto Mañaois' lawyer. He alleged that the victim had been tortured in custody.[22] He also stated that Jacinto Mañaois had received death threats from one of the police interrogators. Relatives submitted a formal request to the NBI to intervene in the case. The initial findings of the NBI investigation indicated that the death may indeed have resulted from police brutality. The NBI also found that the motive for the killing may have been the victim's alleged political sympathies. Amnesty International wrote to the Secretary of National Defense on 20 December 1989, expressing concern at the allegations of torture and the death in custody of Jacinto Mañaois. No substantive reply was received from the authorities.

The CHR initially upheld police claims that Jacinto Mañaois had been killed in a shooting incident after he had grabbed and fired a police officer's gun. However, the CHR subsequently stated that the "killing was evidently a rub-out or summary execution." Charges were filed against two of the policemen involved in the incident in November 1989, and the alleged perpetrators were placed "under restriction" in the custody of the Homicide Section Chief of the Quezon City Police. To Amnesty International's knowledge, the case was still pending prosecution before the courts in November 1991.

Ruben Medina: 5 February 1990, Bataan

On 5 February 1990 Ruben Medina was taken from a bus at a military checkpoint near Maria Fe and Petronila subdivisions in Orani City, Bataan. According to reports, all male passengers were ordered to get off the bus and Ruben Medina was taken into custody after a CAFGU member pointed him out. PC officials denied that Ruben Medina was being held at the PC headquarters in Balanga, Bataan. Officials from Samal police station subsequently stated that Ruben Medina's body could be found at a funeral parlour in *barangay* Gugo, Samal, Bataan and relatives recovered it there.

Police officials involved in the arrest and detention of Ruben Medina reported to officers at Orani police station that he had tried to grab a gun while under arrest. However, an autopsy report indicated that Ruben Medina had been tortured and that his injuries were so extensive as to cast serious doubt on police accounts of a simple shooting incident. The report stated that Ruben Medina's upper and lower arms had been broken. Twenty eight gunshot wounds were found and the entry points of the bullets were at both the back and front of his body. The back of his head had shattered and there were holes in the buttocks, indicating that bullets had penetrated near his genitals. Moreover, marks on the victim's wrists suggested he had been tied or handcuffed, which would have made it difficult for him to seize a weapon.

The motive for the killing has not been established. Relatives believe that it was linked to Ruben Medina's involvement in the political life of his community, including attendance at mass rallies and participation in lawful political activities. Relatives were reportedly too afraid to demand government intervention but the governor of Bataan raised the case with the military authorities. A CHR investigation concluded that those suspected of the killing should be brought before the courts. However, to Amnesty International's knowledge, no charges have been brought against those suspected of responsibility for the death of Ruben Medina. The Chief of Police in Orani was reportedly still on active service and none of the suspected perpetrators had been arrested by the end of November 1991.

Felipe "Wilson" Leonidas: 28 February 1990, Manila

An active member of an organization working on behalf of the urban poor, Felipe "Wilson" Leonidas "disappeared" after being arrested at a restaurant in Santa Cruz, Manila on 22 February 1990. According to eye-witnesses, approximately six armed men in plain clothes dragged him at gunpoint out of the restaurant to a waiting vehicle which then drove off. On 29 February military authorities reported that Felipe Leonidas had died in his cell. They claimed he had hanged himself, but forensic evidence indicated that he may have been deliberately killed by his captors.

Relatives said that they had searched for Felipe Leonidas at local police stations, hospitals and military detention centres, but that his custody was denied by the authorities. On 28 February Felipe Leonidas arrived at his sister's house, escorted by two members of the military intelligence group from Camp Bago Bantay in *barangay* Pag Asa, Quezon City, Metro Manila. He told his sister that he had decided to cooperate with the military and would remain in their "protective custody". The following day military officials informed relatives that Felipe Leonidas had hanged himself in his cell. The military reportedly offered to pay the funeral expenses.

An autopsy report provided at least two pieces of evidence which suggested that Felipe Leonidas may not have committed suicide: first, the marks on the front of the neck were not typical for cases of suicidal hanging; and second, the marks around the whole of the neck *without* the presence of knot marks were "not compatible" with those caused by suicidal hanging. Relatives filed an official complaint with the CHR on 6 April 1990. A CHR case report dated September 1990 indicated either that military authorities at Camp Bago Bantay had been uncooperative or that the CHR had not performed its duty with sufficient energy. The report reads: "CHR investigators exerted efforts to confer with [the commanding officer] regarding the circumstances of the death of Felipe. Unfortunately, he was not available at that time". No further details on the progress of the investigation have since been made public and to Amnesty International's knowledge no case had been brought before the courts by November 1991.

Trade unionists

Dozens of trade unionists have been victims of human rights violations by government and government-backed forces since 1988, including "disappearance" and extrajudicial execution. The majority have been accused by the authorities of being members of front organizations for the CPP/NPA. Members of the *Kilusang Mayo Uno* (KMU), the May First Movement, and the National Federation of Sugar Workers (NFSW), a KMU-affiliate, have been particularly at risk. The KMU and the NFSW have been among the most active and vocal critics of the present government. Military allegations that KMU/NFSW members are involved with the armed opposition have sometimes served to justify the curtailment of lawful trade union activities. Such allegations have encouraged acts of repression, including serious human rights violations against trade unionists.[23]

Cornelio "Oscar" Tagulao: 7 March 1990, Bataan

Cornelio "Oscar" Tagulao, former chairman of the workers' cultural group SIKLAB, was shot dead on 7 March 1990 in Mariveles, Bataan, by at least three unidentified armed men. He was the brother of Rufo Tagulao, President of the KMU-affiliated Alliance of Democratic Labor Organizations-Central Luzon (ADLO-CL). Oscar Tagulao and other members of the family had previously been threatened with death and harassed by members of the 24th IB of the PA, apparently to put pressure on Rufo Tagulao to discontinue his activities as a labour leader. Relatives believed that Rufo Tagulao was the intended victim of the March 1990 attack and that Oscar Tagulao had been mistaken for his brother.

The armed men in civilian clothing approached Oscar Tagulao from behind as he drove a passenger tricycle near the public market in barangay San Carlos, Mariveles municipality, at about 7.15pm. According to reports, he was shot in the back and in the left thigh with

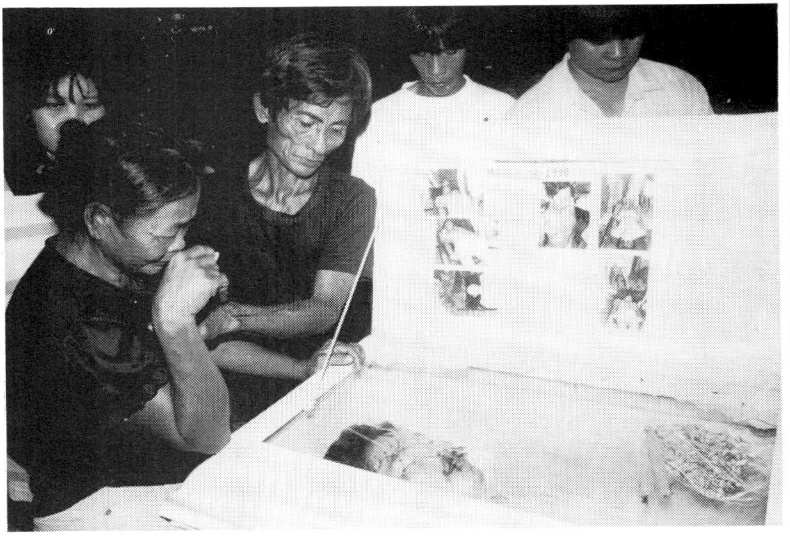

Relatives grieve beside the body of Cornelio "Oscar" Tagulao. He was shot dead in March 1990 by three armed men who apparently mistook him for his brother, Rufo Tagulao, the president of a trade union affiliated to the national "May First Movement" labour union. Oscar was shot in the back and left thigh while driving a passenger tricycle normally used by Rufo. As he lay wounded on the ground, he pleaded with his attackers not to kill him, saying that they had the wrong person. He was then shot at close range and died soon afterwards.

a .45 calibre pistol. Relatives said that Oscar Tagulao was driving a passenger tricycle normally driven by Rufo and was wearing clothing belonging to his brother. As he lay wounded, Oscar pleaded with the men not to kill him, saying that they had the wrong person. He was then shot at close range in the chest and the right shoulder. One of the assailants reportedly shouted: "For every NPA killing, 10 people will be killed in retaliation". On 5 March a CAFGU member had been killed in the area, allegedly by the NPA.

Shortly after Oscar Tagulao's killing, the family met local civilian and military authorities. The local military commander reportedly said that the Tagulao family was on the military's "Order of Battle". He did not confirm or deny that the military was responsible for the killing of Oscar Tagulao but allegedly said he believed it was a "good thing". In a subsequent dialogue, the military commander openly accused the KMU of being a CPP/NPA front and told Rufo Tagulao that as long as he and others remained with the KMU they would continue to have problems from the military.

Oscar Tagulao was killed during a concerted campaign by the 24th IB to weaken several lawful non-governmental organizations which they accused of being "fronts" for the CPP and NPA; among the organizations named was ADLO-CL. On 22 February 1990 Orlando Tagulao — the brother of Oscar and Rufo — was detained by members of the 24th IB and taken to their military detachment in *barangay* Ipag, Mariveles. There he was reportedly interrogated at gunpoint and told to identify local members of the CPP and NPA.

A complaint concerning Oscar Tagulao's murder was filed with the regional office of the CHR but eye-witnesses were reportedly afraid to testify. In July 1991, more than one year after the killing, the CHR reported to Amnesty International that the killing was "apparently a case of mistaken identity" and that it was continuing its investigation. To Amnesty International's knowledge the suspected perpetrators had not been brought before the courts by November 1991.

Hernando Pelaro and Pablito Labrador: 26 January 1990, Negros Occidental

Hernando Pelaro, 16, a farm worker and Pablito Labrador, both members of the NFSW, were shot and killed by named members of the 331st PC Company and a CAFGU unit at about 6am on 26 January 1990. At least three other members of the NFSW, Epifanio Lamada, Antonio Flores and Leonardo Cabansag, were shot in the same incident but survived. The five victims were among a group

The funeral of Herman Evangelista, an organizer for the National Federation of Sugar Workers in Negros. Soldiers shot him dead in July 1990 while he was carrying out a survey of union membership in sugar plantations. © Carol Lee

of about 15 people who were fired upon by members of a CAFGU unit reportedly based at Hacienda Santa Ana, *barangay* Santa Rosa, Murcia, Negros Occidental and led by a PC corporal. Some of the victims were drinking morning coffee in a small village store in Hacienda Alibasao, *barangay* Amayco, Murcia when the shooting occurred, and others were tending their fields nearby.

Eye-witnesses said that the combined PC/CAFGU unit opened fire without warning with M-14 machine guns from a distance of about ten meters, injuring Leonardo Cabansag who was in the store and Epifanio Lamada who was reportedly in a field nearby. The other occupants of the store were then ordered at gunpoint to line up in the street where they were questioned. The store owner was asked about his relationship to some of the other men, including the two who had been wounded. When he replied that they were relatives and neighbours, he was kicked by one of the soldiers identified as the group leader. The soldiers asked why he allowed NPAs to gather at his store and accused his wife of being a member of the NPA herself — an allegation she denied. According to eye-witness reports, when another soldier said: "Sir, they are the ones", the leader pointed his gun at Hernando Pelaro and Pablito Labrador who immediately fell to their knees and begged not to be killed. The soldier then fired his gun killing them instantly. A military helicopter arrived a few minutes later to take the wounded civilians to hospital; the two dead men were left behind.

To Amnesty International's knowledge the suspects identified by eye-witnesses as responsible for the killings had not been charged or disciplined by November 1991.

Herman Evangelista: 6 July 1990, Negros Occidental

Herman Evangelista, aged 26, was shot dead on the afternoon of 6 July 1990 by armed men identified as members of the 7th IB Scout Rangers of the PA. Herman Evangelista was a local organizer and active member of the NFSW.

The military authorities had previously accused Herman Evangelista of being a member of a "front" organization for the outlawed CPP/NPA. In 1989 he was allegedly tortured in military custody. In a sworn affidavit dated 6 November 1989, Herman Evangelista described his arrest, interrogation and torture by members of the 331st PC Company on 16 October 1989. He said that his interrogators insisted that he was working in the underground movement under cover of the NFSW. He reported being hit with the butt of a rifle and punched in different parts of the body. When he asked for water he was given a glass of whisky and urine, and was forced to eat cigarette butts. He was released without charge on 27 October 1989.

On the day of his death, nine months later, Herman Evangelista and a friend were carrying out a survey of union membership in the area of Murcia, Negros Occidental. At Hacienda Limjap they became aware of the presence of armed men and, fearing for their safety, the two union workers left for another hacienda. The man accompanying Herman Evangelista managed to flee to safety, but Herman Evangelista was shot dead by a group of military men who were hiding in a house at the roadside. His body was recovered the following morning by relatives.

At the end of November 1991, Amnesty International was not aware of any official investigation into the death of Herman Evangelista.

Edilberto Bensen, Haydee Bensen and Mary Grace Bensen: 28 August 1991, Negros Occidental

Edilberto Bensen, his pregnant wife Haydee and their 10-year-old daughter Mary Grace were shot by unidentified armed men believed to be members of the 61st IB of the PA on 28 August 1991 in Hacienda Wawa, *barangay* Santa Rosa, Murcia, Negros Occidental. Edilberto and Haydee Bensen were both involved in lawful trade union activities, and this was widely believed to have been the reason for their killings.

A neighbour reported that two masked armed men and about 20

others arrived at the Bensens' home at around 9pm. They ordered Edilberto Bensen to come out. When he did he was met with a heavy burst of gunfire and was wounded in the chest and legs. His wife and daughter rushed downstairs and were also shot. Haydee Bensen's head was said to have been blown off.

Military reports claimed that the family had been killed by NPA members because of Edilberto Bensen's alleged involvement with a local CVO. However, family and friends have denied that Edilberto was a CVO member. Members of the local community believe that trade union membership was more likely to have been the motive for the killings. Edilberto Bensen was a district leader of the NFSW and his wife was a member of the *Kilusang Manggagawa sang Kababayen-an*, the Association of Women Workers. To Amnesty International's knowledge the government had not initiated an official investigation into the killings of the three members of the Bensen family as of November 1991.

Church workers

Priests, nuns and lay members of religious congregations have also been targeted by the military as CPP/NPA sympathizers. One reason is that they have spoken out in defence of the poor and human rights, which the military has tended to interpret as evidence of involvement, either direct or indirect, with the armed insurgency.

The government has appeared at times to reinforce this perception. Government representatives have argued, for example, that the victims of military campaigns or counter-insurgency operations have not been killed because of their religious beliefs or church activities, but because they have engaged in "partisan political activity". Such statements appear to justify the killing of unarmed political activists.They also encourage the view that those whose work leads them to criticize political or social policy are legitimate targets for military campaigns.

Church workers have frequently been threatened with death and a number have been killed by government or government-backed forces. In 1989, the name of Archbishop Antonio Fortich of Bacolod in Negros Occidental appeared on two "hit lists" circulating in Bacolod. The lists were believed to have been distributed by vigilantes and CAFGU members, apparently with the consent and cooperation of local military commanders. One of the lists, signed in the name of Masa Kontra Komunista (the Masses against Communism), began with the words: "These are the lap-dogs of the communists who are leading our brothers astray here in Negros. They have been sentenced to death by the Masses against Communism.[24]

The Reverend Vizminda P Gran and Lovello Gran: 1 May 1989, Misamis Occidental

A 51-year-old minister of the United Church of Christ in the Philippines (UCCP) and human rights advocate, Reverend Vizminda P Gran, was killed on 1 May 1989 along with her husband, Lovello Gran, at their home in *barangay* Del Pilar, Baliangao, Misamis Occidental. They were killed by five masked men. Military authorities initially claimed that thieves were responsible and that a few days later stolen goods were found near the victims' house. However, the military later suggested that the Grans had been killed by the NPA due to an "internal dispute in the underground movement". These allegations were not substantiated.

The Reverend Gran had been labelled as an NPA member by the military authorities and received death threats believed to have originated from security forces and vigilantes. She had also been under surveillance by the military. Her name had appeared on a death list, reportedly compiled with the cooperation of the 44th IB in Calamba, Misamis Occidental, but for which the military later denied responsibility. On 8 June 1989, in a letter to a local human rights lawyer, the anti-communist group *Qrusada su Qalinao Ug Qagawasan,* Crusade for Peace and Freedom, claimed to have killed the Grans for their alleged involvement with communist groups.

Investigations revealed that one of the firearms used in the killing had been issued to a CAFGU member, the brother of the local mayor. The AFP then alleged that the killing was probably politically motivated because The Reverend Gran was "rumoured to have harboured the ambition for mayorship..." In November 1989 the CAFGU member believed to have carried out the killing, and three others, were charged with double murder and robbery. The CAFGU member was arrested in July 1990. Three months later he was released on bail. He was subsequently expelled from the CAFGU but allowed to return to Baliangao.

Both the judicial authorities and witnesses seem to have been subjected to pressure or intimidation by members of the mayor's family. Two of the suspects, who were reportedly willing to appear as witnesses for the prosecution, are believed to have gone into hiding after receiving reports that the 44th IB had targeted them for elimination. Amnesty International wrote to the government in May 1991 and requested information about the progress of official investigation of the deaths of the Grans. The government has to date provided no information in reply to Amnesty international's inquiries. The case was still pending before the court in Oroquieta City, Misamis Occidental in November 1991.

Father Narciso Pico: 10 January 1991, Negros Occidental

Father Narciso Pico, a 42-year-old parish priest of the Philippine Independent Church (PIC), was shot dead on 10 January 1991 by two armed men believed to be CAFGU members in *barangay* Antipoli, Pontevedra, Negros Occidental.[25]

Father Pico had gone to a cafeteria with three young members of his parish. As they rose to leave, two men, one of whom was reportedly wearing a camouflage outfit, began shooting at Father Narciso. He was hit in the shoulder and back. An eye-witness reported that he cried out: "My God! have pity, enough". One of the gunmen said "finish him off". The second is then reported to have fired at the priest's head at close range.

Father Narciso Pico was 42 years old and a native of Negros Occidental province. He was a parish priest in Antipolo and was active in a number of religious and human rights organizations, including the Promotion of Church People's Rights (PCPR). Father Pico reportedly advocated land reform and was said to have preached against the Sugar Development Fund (SDF), established by sugar planters in 1988. The SDF has provided funds for the maintenance of special CAFGU forces stationed on sugar plantations and privately owned estates and industries in Negros. Father Pico had argued that the planters used the special CAFGUs to intimidate those advocating land reform and greater social justice.

During the years before his death Father Pico had received a series of warnings and veiled threats which were believed to have emanated from military sources. In July 1989 Father Pico was accused on television of being an NPA "organizer", an accusation he dismissed as a "blatant lie". The television statement was made by an unidentified "rebel-returnee", a former NPA guerrilla captured by or "surrendered" to the military forces[26].

In April 1991 the CHR submitted a resolution to the *Fiscal* (public prosecutor) asking for murder charges to be filed against two suspected killers of Narciso Pico. In its resolution, the CHR

© Carol Lee

Church workers have frequently been threatened with death and a number have been killed by government or government-backed forces. Archbishop Antonio Fortich (left) has been threatened with death on several occasions. In 1989 his name appeared on two "hitlists" believed to have been distributed by vigilantes apparently with the cooperation of military commanders in Negros.

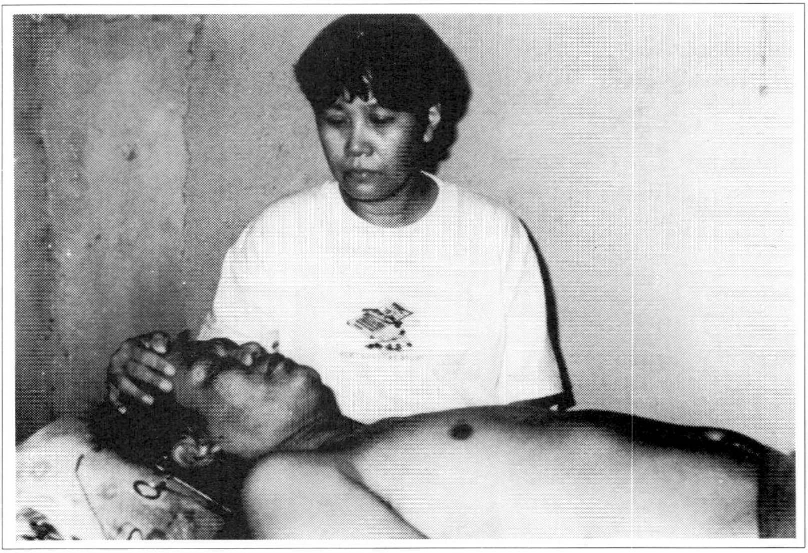

Father Narciso Pico was shot dead in January 1991 by two armed men identified as a vigilante and a CAFGU member. He was first wounded, then one of the gunmen shouted "finish him off", and the other shot him in the head at close range. Father Pico had been active in several religious and human rights organizations, and had advocated land reform and greater social justice.

said it had found three witnesses who had signed affidavits identifying the alleged killers. One of the alleged killers was a "rebel-returnee", who had joined an anti-communist organization called the Brotherhood of Organized Returnees in Negros (BORN). The CHR also stated that this suspect was connected with BAC-UP 3, a police precinct in Bacolod City, and that he was apparently being protected by the police. In response to the CHR report, the Provincial PNP Superintendent reportedly told bishops and clergymen from the PIC that he did not know the identity of the suspects or that they were under police protection.

Murder charges against the suspected "rebel-returnee" were filed by the Negros provincial Fiscal on 3 July 1991 with a recommendation of no bail and a warrant of arrest was issued by the courts. On 25 July the suspect reportedly surrendered and was taken into the custody of the PNP in Hinigaran, Negros Occidental. However, on August the suspected killer of Narciso Pico was granted bail by a judge at the Regional Trial Court of La Carlota City and released from detention.

To Amnesty International's knowledge there have been no further arrests in connection with this case and the suspected killers remain at large.

Human rights lawyers

Since 1987 at least six human rights lawyers have been killed, apparently because of their human rights activities or their defence of suspects in political cases. All had received death threats before being murdered.A seventh human rights lawyer, Vidal Tombo, narrowly escaped death on 17 July 1991, when he was shot in the stomach and arm by gunmen believed to be linked with the security forces. The majority of the murdered lawyers were members of the Free Legal Assistance Group (FLAG), a network of human rights lawyers which provides free legal aid to disadvantaged groups and legal counsel for defendants in political cases. Dozens of human rights lawyers in the Philippines have received death threats. The names of some have also appeared on lists of alleged CPP/NPA supporters compiled by military and police authorities.[27]

Attorney Alfonso "Al" Surigao: 24 June 1988, Cebu

Attorney Alfonso Surigao, a leading human rights lawyer in Cebu City, was shot dead on 24 June 1988 after three armed men burst into his house in Tabocanal, Pardo, Cebu City.[28] Prior to his death, both Alfonso Surigao and his wife had been under military surveillance and had been subjected to harassment by military personnel. Attorney Surigao had also received death threats throughout 1987 and early 1988. These threats were reportedly repeated in the week before he was killed.

His killing in June 1988 was widely believed to have been directly linked to his defence of a group of 26 farmers from Leyte. They had been arrested after publicizing human rights violations by vigilante groups. The 26, all of whom Amnesty International considered prisoners of conscience, were arrested in Manila in November 1987, accused of being NPA supporters. They were brought to trial in Cebu City on charges of rebellion and other acts of violence.[29]

After Attorney Surigao's death the Cebu police publicly stated that their investigation had met with "a blank wall", although eyewitnesses had described the killers. A few days after the killing the National Chief of the PC claimed that: "Surigao's killers were the [communist] rebels themselves; it is somewhat an inside job". On 28 June 1988 Alfonso Surigao's brother said witnesses had signed affidavits testifying that the director of Regional Security Unit (RSU) 7, a

Attorney Alfonso "Al" Surigao, a leading human rights lawyer, was shot dead in July 1988 in his house by three armed men believed to be backed by a military intelligence unit. At the time of his death he was defending 26 farmers arrested after publicizing human rights violations by pro-government vigilante groups in Leyte. They were later charged with rebellion and other crimes. At least five other human rights lawyers have been killed in similar circumstances since 1987.

military intelligence agency, had threatened Attorney Surigao several times. The NBI took responsibility for the investigation on 29 June.

On 11 July 1988 a "military asset"[30] surrendered to the authorities and confessed that he had killed Attorney Surigao. He claimed that the director of RSU 7 had suggested to him that Attorney Surigao should be killed and had paid him 500 pesos after the murder had been committed. The vigilante was convicted of murder and sentenced to life imprisonment on 14 February 1989. As far as Amnesty International is aware, the two other suspects have been identified but have not been arrested.

Charges against the director of RSU 7 were initially filed in a military court, but President Aquino waived military jurisdiction over the case in September 1988. The RSU director was relieved of his duties and placed under "technical arrest"[31] in a military camp in Cebu, where the man suspected of having carried out the killing was also detained. Under these conditions the suspected murderer withdrew his allegations against the director of RSU 7. In November 1988 charges against the director were dropped. In June 1990 the director was again charged with the murder of Alfonso Surigao, but he was released from detention after posting bail in July 1990. He was subsequently reassigned to another RSU unit in Misamis Oriental. In September 1990 members of the RSU unit in Misamis Oriental were believed to have been responsible for death threats against FLAG lawyer Oscar Musni, acting as counsel for the Surigao family.

The trial of the RSU 7 director began in January 1991, but further information on the progress of the case has not been made public. To Amnesty International's knowledge the suspect remained on active service at the end of November 1991.

Attorney Oscar E Tonog: 21 March 1989, Northern Samar

Oscar E Tonog, a human rights lawyer, was gunned down by two unidentified men on 21 March 1989 in Catarman, Northern Samar. He died the following day. He was an active member of FLAG and Vice-President of the Northern Samar chapter of the Integrated Bar of the Philippines.[32]

According to eye-witnesses, on 21 March between 5pm and 6pm Oscar Tonog was driving his motorcycle with his wife sitting behind. It began to rain and he slowed down to seek shelter. As he did so a man shot Oscar Tonog at point blank range in the cheek, left breast and back. The man escaped with an accomplice on a motorcycle. Oscar Tonog died at about 10pm on 22 March.

At the time of his murder, Oscar Tonog was defending one of two suspected NPA members. He had secured 40,000 pesos for his client's bail but the military then imposed additional charges on the suspect. At around the same time an announcer on a local radio station, who was believed to have links with the military intelligence service, warned all human rights lawyers that "their day was near". It was also reported that members of a vigilante group known as the Northern Samar Anti-Communist Alliance (NORSACA), organized by a military lieutenant, had pinned up posters claiming credit for the killing of Oscar Tonog.

Several people witnessed the killing but none was willing to come forward as they apparently feared military reprisals. Nevertheless, the NBI drew a sketch of the killer with the help of Oscar Tonog's widow. A Philippine Government representative stated before the 46th session of the UN Commission on Human Rights in February 1990, more than one year after the incident:

> "*That no one has been arrested nor charged yet for the murder of Attorney Tonog is technically true. But the arrest of the alleged killer could be at any time now*".

He confirmed that the CHR had identified the alleged killer of Oscar Tonog, and stated that the suspect's hiding place in Manila was under surveillance by the NBI. However, no charges had been filed against the suspected killers of Oscar Tonog and no arrests had been made in connection with this case by November 1991. Despite the fact that the killing was witnessed by several people, the authorities have apparently failed to provide proper protection to witnesses to enable them to testify. Those suspected of killing Oscar Tonog were believed to be still at large in November 1991, nearly three years after the murder was committed.

Suspected members of the armed opposition

A number of those killed by government forces have been suspected NPA members. Military and police authorities have sought to justify the killings by claiming that the victims were killed during an armed encounter or while the victims were resisting arrest. However, in many cases eyewitness testimony, often corroborated by both official and independent investigations, has provided evidence that the security forces opened fire on unarmed civilians. These killings give rise to serious concern for at least two reasons. First, extrajudicial execution can never serve as an alternative to the arrest of those suspected of criminal offences by the authorities. Where the victims are unarmed the killings are absolutely unjustifiable. Second, military or police allegations of NPA membership are known to have been extended to include many people whose lawful social or political activities have been deemed unacceptable by the security forces. Under these conditions the risk of people who have taken no part in unlawful activities becoming victims of political killings is especially great.

Norman and Antonio Akien: 3 April 1990, Mountain Province

Two brothers, Norman and Antonio Akien, were reportedly detained and shot by members of the 194th PC Company at barangay Kayan, Tadian, Mountain Province on 3 April 1990. Norman Akien was a university student in Baguio and Antonio Akien was alleged to have been a medical officer with the NPA. Both had returned home on the previous day to celebrate Easter with their family.

According to eye-witnesses, the brothers, both unarmed, were detained by PC soldiers as they sat talking in a rice field near their home. They were dragged to some other PC soldiers, some of whom have been identified by name. Norman Akien was reportedly shot in the stomach, the heart and the head while being held by two soldiers. Before he was killed, witnesses heard Norman Akien cry out that he was a civilian. Antonio Akien was reportedly held and punched in the face before being shot several times.

Two days later, members of the community decided to stage an "indignation rally" outside the 194th PC Company detachment at Babalaan, Tadian. Military authorities from the detachment subsequently claimed in an open letter that Norman and Antonio Akien had died in an armed encounter. They portrayed the reports of *barangay* officials, human rights groups and relatives as "baseless, bias [sic] and unfounded" and a "smear campaign to tarnish the good image earned by the [194th PC] company".

A military report by an officer of the 194th PC Company, dated 5 April 1990, indicated that the raid was intended primarily to intimidate the local community which was believed to be sympathetic to "anti-government elements". It stated that:

> *"In the final analysis the operation was conducted...so as to show the populace that coddling anti-government elements would only make their lives miserable..."*

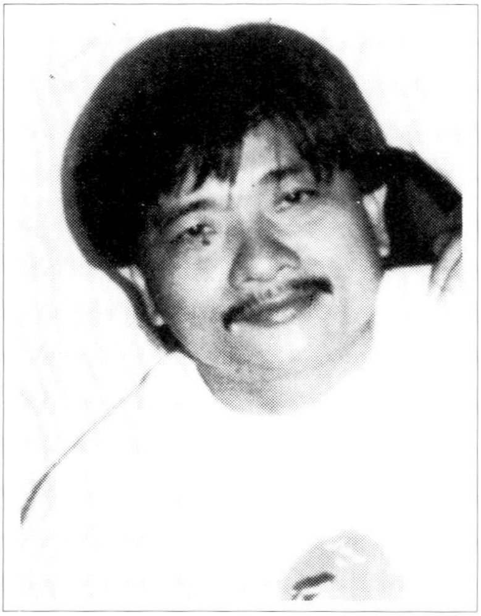

Jose "Bong" Concepcion died in December 1990 after being shot in the head at point blank range while at a store picking up groceries. His attackers were believed to be members of the 24th Infantry Battalion (IB) of the Philippine Army. In September 1990, three months before he was killed, a military officer reportedly asked him to become a military informer, but he refused. An officer from the 24th IB later told a mass meeting that Jose Concepcion's community activities were a cover for illegal political activities.

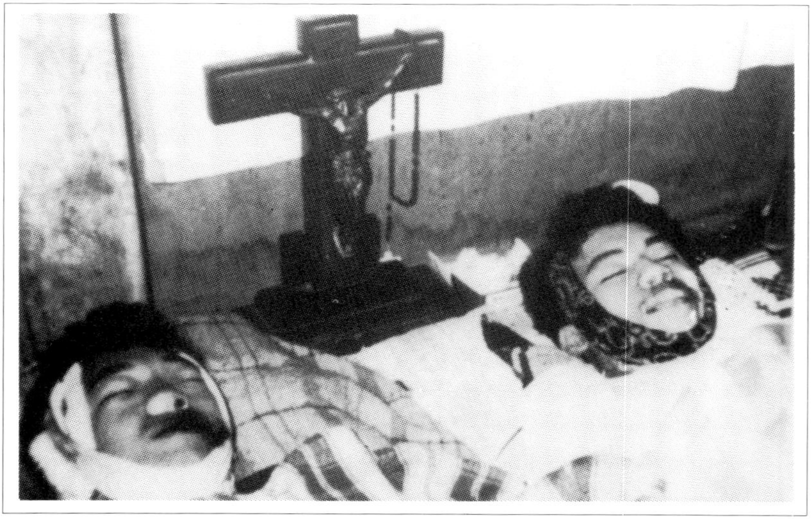

Norman and Antonio Akien were shot dead by members of the Philippine Constabulary in April 1990. The brothers had just returned to their home village to celebrate Easter with their family. Norman was a university student; Antonio was alleged to be a member of the New People's Army opposition group. They were sitting talking in a rice field when soldiers arrived and dragged them away. Eye-witnesses said that Norman was shot in the stomach, heart and head while being held down and Antonio was punched in the face before being shot several times.

The CHR published an initial case report in mid-1990. It stated that once the evidence had been compiled a hearing would be conducted to enable both the military and the witnesses to present their version of events to the CHR. Some months later, however, it was reported that a hearing scheduled for November 1990 had been postponed because the CHR had failed to properly inform the witnesses and suspected perpetrators of the arrangements for the hearing.

Since then no further details of the investigations by the authorities have been made public. By November 1991, nearly two years after the deaths of the Akien brothers, no charges were believed to have been brought against the suspected killers and no arrests had been made in connection with the case.

Jose Dy and Gilberto Lopez: 28 June 1990, Metro Manila

On 28 June 1990 PC members violently assaulted participants at a funeral march for an alleged NPA member. The attack resulted in the deaths of two of the mourners, Jose Dy and Gilberto Lopez. A dozen or so more were injured. Witnesses said that the mourners had just entered the cemetery in La Loma, Caloocan City, Metro Manila when about 20 armed men, some of them wearing masks, appeared. The assailants were identified as members of the PC Capital Command and the Caloocan City police. After ordering the procession to stop, at least five of them opened fire with M-16 rifles and handguns. Immediately after the shooting, 21 mourners were arrested, taken to the Caloocan City police headquarters and charged with inciting sedition. The charges were dismissed by the courts on 19 January 1991.

A PC commander subsequently claimed that the deaths had occurred during a legitimate encounter. He stated in press interviews that PC troops were "on an authorized mission to arrest rebels" and that his men had worn masks to avoid being recognized by NPA members. He was also reported to have stated that the murders could be a "deterrent" to further displays of sedition. The soldiers involved claimed that when the mourners had entered the cemetery they unfurled a red flag, shouted revolutionary slogans and attempted to throw one or two grenades at the policemen. However, witnesses, including journalists, said no grenades were seen or found.

The Director General of the PNP subsequently formed a panel to investigate the incident and an internal police report called the incident "an eloquent picture of police and military brutality". In July 1990 the CHR initiated an investigation and hearings and, in

May 1991, found a *prima facie* case for murder which they referred to the prosecutor's office. The CHR recommended that charges be filed against the two PC officers alleged to have been responsible for the incident. Despite this apparently prompt and effective response by the authorities, no charges are in fact believed to have been brought against those believed responsible for the funeral killings. To Amnesty International's knowledge, the suspects remained at large at the end of November 1991.

Amnesty International addressed an urgent telex to President Aquino on 4 July 1990. The telex expressed concern at the killings, urged the government to conduct an immediate investigation and asked to be kept informed of its progress. No substantive reply was received to this or to a further request for information sent in May 1991 to the Department of National Defense and the CHR.[33]

Jose "Bong" M Concepcion Jr: 16 December 1990, Pampanga

On 16 December 1990 Jose "Bong" M Concepcion Jr was killed outside his store in *barangay* Roxas, Mabalacat, Pampanga by two men in civilian clothes believed to be members of the 24th IB of the PA.

Jose Concepcion and his wife were preparing a meal when he left the house and went to the family's store to get some cooking oil. Armed men reportedly appeared in front of him as he reached the store and shot him at point blank range in the cheek. Neighbours rushed him to hospital but he died within 15 minutes of being shot. A doctor took a .45 calibre bullet from his head and estimated he had been shot from a range of three feet.

Jose Concepcion had previously been arrested in 1986 with Rodolfo Salas, a prominent trade unionist and NDF leader. The arrest of Jose Concepcion was linked to his alleged activities as driver and security aide to Rodolfo Salas and one other NDF leader. Jose Concepcion was released from detention after relatives filed a petition for a writ of *habeas corpus.* His trial on charges of rebellion was continuing at the time of his death.

After his release from custody in 1986, Jose Concepcion became involved in community activities within his local *barangay*. He assisted in the construction of a basketball court and was known for his strong concern for youth and his participation in an anti-drug campaign.

In September 1990 a military detachment of the 24th IB of the PA was established in *barangay* Mabalacat. Jose Concepcion was reportedly approached by a military officer and asked to become a military informer. He was said to have refused and to have stated that he wished to lead a normal life. The 24th IB of the PA called a mass meeting at which a Major reportedly told those present that Jose Concepcion's involvement in the life of the *barangay* was a cover for his unlawful political activities. The day before his death Jose Concepcion had told his wife that he was being watched and followed by unidentified gunmen.

Investigations into the killing of Jose Concepcion were conducted by CHR, the NBI and the local police, but the progress or outcome of these investigations has not been made public. To Amnesty International's knowledge no arrests had been made in connection with the killing of Jose Concepcion by the end of November 1991.

4

Killings by armed opposition groups

In recent years NPA members are alleged to have committed numerous acts of violence and these have included the torture and execution of CPP/NPA members accused of spying for the military; and the killing of members of rural communities, trade unionists involved in labour disputes and members of the civilian administration.

The killings are human rights abuses which have been committed in violation of humanitarian law as outlined in Chapter 1. The leadership of the CPP/NPA, represented publicly by the National Democratic Front (NDF), has in some instances apologized for incidents of abuse and has announced that disciplinary measures have been taken against the suspected perpetrators. The government has also conducted investigations into reports of human rights abuses by members of opposition groups and details of these are referred to where appropriate.

Killings within the NPA

Among the most serious human rights abuses reportedly committed by the NPA are abductions and summary executions which apparently occurred during the course of at least two separate "purges" within the CPP/NPA. Individuals suspected of being military informers who had infiltrated the NPA were reportedly "tried" by unofficial courts and summarily executed, some after being tortured. The first such purge, which received widespread publicity in the national media, is believed to have taken place in Mindanao during 1985. Hundreds of people may have been killed by the NPA during this period, although the actual number of victims has never been properly verified.

Evidence of executions within the NPA emerged in late 1988 when documents were seized from a CPP agent arrested by the government in November. The documents reportedly outlined a CPP/NPA plan, codenamed "Operation Missing Link", for action between April and November 1988. Its objective was to root out suspected "deep penetration agents" (DPAs), government agents believed to have infiltrated the party. The captured documents were also reported to reveal that three of the more than 50 people who reportedly "disappeared" in 1988 had been abducted by the NPA.

In December 1988 three NPA members who surrendered or were captured by government forces alleged that the CPP/NPA had been responsible for the imprisonment, torture and execution of other members of the organization, and suggested that many of the victims were not spies but loyal party members. Apolinario Pabricio, a member of a guerrilla unit of the NPA, said that he and three other members of his unit suspected of being DPAs, had been taken against their will by NPA members to a detention camp in Quezon on 17 November 1988, where they were hit with rifle butts and held in huts chained to stretchers. He said that he "confessed" to being a DPA after three weeks and was subsequently released from detention. Eduardo Borromeo described being detained by the NPA on 19 October 1988 and held in the same camp as Apolinario Pabricio. He alleged he was chained and kept in a small bamboo cage and hung by the wrists from a tree for hours on end. The two claimed to have escaped execution when the leadership of the NDF called a halt to the killings on 1 November 1988.

A third NPA member, Severino Ranoda, said that he surrendered to the military authorities in October 1988, after learning that he had been named as a DPA by Eduardo Borromeo. He said that he had been assigned to the task force responsible for carrying out "Operation Missing Link" and learned of the executions while guarding a rebel camp in Laguna. Severino Ranoda also reported witnessing one killing, when a six-man group beat an NPA member with a crow bar and then stabbed him to death with a bayonet.

In May 1989 the three former NPA members led military forces to four graves in Quezon and Laguna provinces. A military document reported the discovery of 48 bodies, although the skeletal remains of only 12 bodies had actually been exhumed by mid-1989. Other graves have since reportedly been discovered in Pampanga, Sorsogon, Negros Occidental and Misamis Oriental provinces although it is not known whether these in fact contain the remains of victims of "Operation Missing Link".

The precise nature of actions explicitly authorized by "Operation Missing Link" remain unknown and it has not been possible to obtain independent verification of testimony provided by NPA members after capture by or surrender to the military authorities. However it is widely believed that a breakdown in party discipline occurred and resulted in killings by the NPA of an estimated 40 to 60 NPA members during 1988.[34] The NDF leadership is believed to have put a stop to such executions in November 1988.

Members of rural communities

During the past three years there have been several reports of shooting incidents involving the NPA which have resulted in the death of unarmed civilians in rural communities. The victims have included men, women and children and in at least two cases known to Amnesty International they have been members of religious communities. Evidence suggests that some of the killings may have been carried out because the members of a particular community had shifted their allegiance from the NPA to the government.

Fourteen people, including six children, were reportedly killed in August 1989 when NPA members fired on their homes in Dipalog, Misamis Occidental. The adult victims were believed to have been former NPA supporters. On 16 October 1991 four people were reportedly killed and several others wounded at *barangay* Del Monte, Talacogon town, Agusan del Sur when suspected NPA members opened fire on villagers. The victims were leaders of the *Itumans* "the Black Ones", a religious sect. During the 1980s the military was believed to have deployed *Ituman* groups in counter-insurgency operations in the Mindanao region.

One of the most widely documented and publicized of such incidents happened at Digos, Davao del Sur, on 25 June 1989. A group of NPA members killed some 37 people in and around a house near a UCCP chapel in *sitio* Rano, *barangay* Binaton, Digos, Davao del Sur. Most of the victims were unarmed women and children. Two were beheaded.

Military authorities initially reported that NPA members had fired directly at the unarmed victims. The UCCP and the NDF conducted separate investigations into the case. According to the

NDF, the insurgents had gone to Digos to settle differences between the NPA and the *Itumans*, as there were numerous family ties between the two groups. However, the NPA members did not employ intermediaries, as was customary, but confronted the local *Ituman* leader with a heavily armed NPA group. The NDF report stated that a villager hiding in the house had opened fire and in the gun battle that followed 37 people died. It claimed that the NPA members could not see who was inside the house. The UCCP report confirmed that some of the victims had been armed and stated that some had been killed inside the house.

The NDF and UCCP reports both indicated that the killings were linked to the *Itumans'* alleged involvement in counter-insurgency activities supported by the military. The residents of *sitio* Rano had previously supported the NPA and two community leaders were said to have been NPA organizers for some years. In 1986 the residents became members of the UCCP. In the same year military forces and members of the local anti-communist vigilante group the *Pulahans,* "The Red Ones", reportedly began to harass and intimidate residents of Rano. A community leader was arrested and forced to confess to links with the NPA and identify other NPA members.

In July 1989 the UCCP addressed both the NDF and the government. It deplored the violence perpetrated by members of the NPA, but noted that:

> *"We have received reports...that the Armed Forces of the Philippines has been using some of our churches and chapels as bases of operation. Our pastors tell us that rural congregations have been organized into anti-communist vigilante units and fanatical cults. Worse yet, government forces have armed these groups, using them as instruments in their counter-insurgency effort."*

The NDF subsequently reported that it had ordered both the NPA commanding officers and those believed responsible to be brought to "trial". They were accused of carrying out a military action which posed a threat to the lives of unarmed women and children. One year later, the NDF declared in a letter to the UCCP that "corrective and disciplinary measures" had been administered to those who had committed the "infraction", but did not provide details of the measures. The nature of NDF disciplinary procedures remains unclear.

Trade unionists

Violence has marked labour relations in the Philippines at all levels. Both the official security forces and unofficial armed groups acting with their cooperation have been implicated in numerous human rights violations, including summary executions of trade unionists and other workers. NPA urban assassination squads or "sparrow units" have also used violence in relation to labour disputes, including the killing members of labour unions seen as opposed to the CPP/NPA.

Between October and December 1990, at least three trade union leaders and activists were shot dead, apparently by NPA hit squads. Press and other sources suggested that the victims were killed because the *Lakas Manggagawa Labor Center* (LMLC), had refused to join general strikes led by more militant unions in October and December.

On 22 October 1990 unidentified armed men shot dead Oscar Lazaro. He was President of the *Pasang Masda* drivers' federation, which was believed to have refused to join a planned general strike. A CHR report received by Amnesty International in July 1991 stated that witnesses had identified three of the four men responsible for the death of Oscar Lazaro as members of the "sparrow unit", the Alex Boncayao Brigade. All four were reportedly still at large, although a case for murder had been filed at the office of the Rizal Provincial Prosecutor.

In December 1990, two other union leaders were killed — Eduardo Federico, President of the Democratic and Independent Workers' Association (DIWA); and Ernesto Gonzales, Treasurer of the Commercial and Agro-Industrial Labor Organizations (CAILO). Both were killed at approximately 11.30am on 10 December 1990. Three unidentified armed men entered an LMLC conference at the Ateneo de Manila University campus in Quezon City. Witnesses said that one man acted as a lookout while two others burst into the conference hall and opened fire. They were carrying a .45 calibre pistol and an armalite rifle. A third union activist was wounded during the incident. Eduardo Federico sustained eight gunshot wounds and died instantly. Ernesto Gonzales was hit three times in the chest and died on arrival at a nearby hospital.

Government officials

Government officials, including mayors, town councillors and *barangay* captains have been among those killed by NPA "sparrow units" and regular guerrilla units in recent years. In some cases the victims were known for their anti-communist views and opposition to the CPP/NPA. Other victims of NPA shootings have included the children and relatives of police or militia officials, or civilians with no connection to the government, who have been killed during ambush attacks or assaults on their homes.

Rodolfo Trinidad, a town councillor in Valenzuela, Metro Manila, was killed by suspected NPA members while on his way to work on 5 July 1989. He died instantly from several wounds when his car was riddled with bullets from automatic pistols at around 9am. According to his wife, Rodolfo Trinidad had been receiving death threats from the NPA since 1987, when his car had also been sprayed with bullets. In Surigao del Sur, Jose Sulima, also a town mayor, was shot dead by suspected NPA members while walking with relatives on 14 September 1989. Jose Sulima was reportedly known for his staunch anti-communist views.

A former town mayor, Cerilio Cariaga, and at least three others were killed when armed men believed to be NPA members fired upon a group seeking to hold a peace dialogue with the insurgents in *barangay* San Roque, Bato, Camarines Sur on 13 May 1991. A PNP director said the six-person team, comprising of two policemen and four civilian volunteers, was planning to negotiate the surrender of a local NPA commander when they were fired upon by NPA members reportedly belonging to another guerrilla unit operating in the province.

Amnesty International condemns the deliberate and arbitrary killing of civilians or prisoners. It believes that all parties to internal armed conflict are bound by humanitarian law. It urges the NPA to refrain from such acts of violence and to abide by the terms and standards of common Article 3 of the Geneva Conventions.

5

The problem of impunity

Members of the security forces have committed extrajudicial executions with impunity despite the Government's stated commitment to the protection of human rights and the substantial legal and constitutional guarantees of these rights. According to available information, only two members of the official security forces, two military "assets" and two former members of the CHDF have been sentenced to prison terms for extrajudicial executions committed since January 1986.[35] None has been convicted in military courts. This chapter seeks to clarify why so few of those suspected of committing extrajudicial executions have been brought to justice. It examines the existing mechanisms for investigating human rights violations and for prosecuting suspected perpetrators. The factors impeding the full and impartial investigation of alleged extrajudicial executions and the prosecution of the suspected perpetrators may be summarized as follows:

- the quasi-judicial procedures used by the CHR have tended to make witnesses and complainants vulnerable to retribution without offering them any of the advantages of a real judicial proceeding;
- the CHR and, to a lesser extent, the civil courts have tended to accept without question the testimony of members of the security forces in cases of alleged unlawful killings;
- military courts have, until recently, had exclusive jurisdiction over cases involving members of the security forces, regardless of the nature of the alleged offence;
- military and police investigations have often been conducted by those in command of the suspected perpetrators;

- members of the security forces have refused to cooperate with, or have actively obstructed, the course of investigation and prosecution;
- a lack of clarity in defining the respective responsibilities of the various investigative and prosecutorial agencies has meant that agencies often fail to take full responsibility for cases, preferring to "endorse" them to another agency for final resolution;
- witnesses, complainants, defence lawyers and members of the judiciary involved in human rights cases have been routinely subjected to intimidation and some have been killed, with the result that many have been afraid to become involved for fear of reprisals;
- provisions for witness protection have been inadequate.

In Amnesty International's experience, where conviction of those responsible for human rights violations is exceptional rather than usual, the perpetrators of extrajudicial executions and other serious human rights violations inevitably come to believe that they are beyond the reach of the law. By failing to ensure that the perpetrators of extrajudicial executions are brought to justice, the government effectively condones the practice which can then lead to its perpetuation.

The failure to convict

The government has consistently claimed that a substantial number of military and police officers have been brought to justice for extrajudicial executions. However, despite requests by Amnesty International, it has failed to provide sufficiently detailed evidence of such convictions. The absence of public records concerning conviction for serious human rights violations and the near silence of the authorities when asked to demonstrate their efforts to bring suspected perpetrators to justice, contribute to the widely held perception that, with respect to human rights violations, the military and police forces in the Philippines are beyond the reach of the law.

In a statement to the Human Rights Committee in April 1989, the government said that there had been "six officers and soldiers found guilty for human rights violations and they are discharged from service or reprimanded." The government cited three cases as examples: "Captain Ochote was reprimanded in view of maltreatment; Sergeant Orial was demoted in rank for maltreatment; and Sergeant Paguiderman was meted one year suspension without pay." However, the three officers had apparently not yet been tried. As the government statement explained, their "...being discharged does not mean that they are already exempted. On the contrary they still face proper complaint filed against them." It is noteworthy that none of the three appeared on later government lists of officers convicted of human rights offenses. The government did not provide any information about the other three who it claimed had been "found guilty" of human rights violations.

In 1991 the Department of National Defense reported that of 173 human rights complaints against members of the INP, and 172 against members of the AFP, only 13 had resulted in convictions. A list called "Human Rights Violation Resulting To Conviction: January 1989-1990" included 12 cases of murder or homicide and one case of "threats". The list provided few details of the circumstances in which the crimes were committed, making it difficult to confirm whether the convictions were, in fact, for human rights related offenses as opposed to common crimes. There were several indications that they were for the latter. None of the victims listed was among the more than 550 people known to have been extrajudicially executed between 1988 and 1991. Moreover, the victims in at least three of the 13 cases were themselves members of the security forces, and therefore self-evidently not civilians killed in extrajudicial executions.[36] Finally, information from other sources indicates that at least one case of multiple murder and frustrated murder cited in the list was not a politically motivated extrajudicial execution but a common crime.[37]

In a detailed response to Amnesty International's June 1991 report on violations against trade unionists, the Department of Labor and Employment provided another list of "Convictions in Human Rights Cases".[38] This was apparently based on CHR records and cited 15 cases. Oddly, the cases were not the same as those in the Department of National Defense list. Nine of the cases involved allegations of murder or homicide, and of these three were said to have resulted in prison sentences. Again, insufficient information was provided to determine whether these convictions were for extrajudicial executions as properly defined, or for common crimes. Given the CHR's very broad interpretation of the term "human rights violations", there is reason to believe that some, if not all, were of the latter category.

A government list received by Amnesty International in 1990 and again in 1991 named 42 police and military personnel convicted of "serious human rights violations" from 1986 to 1990. Only 14 cases involved crimes committed after the change of government in 1986. Of all the cases, 33 involved allegations of murder or homicide and six were related to frustrated homicide or murder. Once again, the information was insufficient to determine whether these convictions were in fact for extrajudicial executions. The possibility remained that the convictions were for common crimes. A letter from a Philippine Government representative accompanying the list said: "I hope that this list will disprove the allegation that the military commit human rights violations in the Philippines with "impunity" because they know they can get away with it, which is not the case..."

Amnesty International wrote to the Department of National Defense in May 1991 to seek further clarification about the cases on the various lists, but received no reply. A similar letter written to the CHR was answered but the CHR provided no information on prosecutions and convictions of security force personnel. In her letter, the CHR Chairman said that she regretted that "...this Commission cannot provide very accurate information on this matter since all offenses, with very few exceptions...are triable by courts martial." Amnesty International wrote again to the CHR on 27 August 1991 reiterating its request for detailed information on more than 100 outstanding cases of extrajudicial execution. It expressed concern that the CHR was unable to provide information on the prosecution and conviction of security force personnel for human rights related offences.[39]

Amnesty International has independently obtained information concerning a handful of successful prosecutions for apparent extrajudicial executions by members of government and government-backed forces committed after 1986. Only two of these convictions involved police or military suspects; the rest were former members of official militia forces or hired civilian hitmen known as "military assets".

- On 27 October 1989 the Supreme Court reportedly confirmed a 12-year prison sentence for two police officers convicted of killing B Curallo, an NPA suspect, in Camarines Sur in March 1986. The Court ruled that the victim's position as an NPA commander did not justify his extrajudicial execution by the police.

- A "military asset", Alan Climaco, charged with the June 1988 murder of human rights lawyer Alfonso Surigao, was convicted and sentenced to life imprisonment in February 1989. After many delays a PC officer, Major Palcuto, alleged to have ordered the killing, was charged with murder. His trial began in January 1991 but he posted bail in July 1991. To Amnesty International's knowledge, he was not dismissed from military service and was subsequently assigned to another region.
- In April 1991 the Regional Trial Court in Malaybalay, Bukidnon, convicted two former CHDF members for the killing of George Bahian, a suspected rebel sympathizer, in *sitio* Magsal, *barangay* Guinoyoran, Valencia, Bukidnon on 30 December 1988.
- In November 1989 Sagin Monday was found guilty of homicide by the Regional Trial Court in Koronadal, South Cotabato, for the April 1988 killing of Father Carl Schmitz, a 70-year-old United States citizen. Although it was unclear whether the killing was politically motivated, there was evidence that Sagin Monday had been acting with the support of PC officials.

The problem of impunity has also been evident in a few highly publicized cases. In these the suspected perpetrators of extrajudicial executions have been exonerated following investigations or acquitted by the courts, in spite of substantial eye-witness and circumstantial evidence of their guilt.

One of the most notorious cases in recent years was the acquittal in July 1989 of those believed responsible for the "Lupao massacre" of 11 February 1987. Seventeen civilians, including six children and a couple in their eighties, were reportedly killed by soldiers in revenge for an NPA attack on their unit.[40] The military initially said that the 17 had been "killed in cross-fire". Eye-witnesses and subsequent investigations rejected this claim, saying that the villagers had been deliberately killed by the soldiers of the 14th IB. Nonetheless, the effort to "whitewash" the case continued through the trial process. The Lawyers Committee for Human Rights summarized the outcome of the trial by military court in the following terms:

> *Although eye-witnesses to the crime provided compelling evidence linking specific defendants to the crime, all were acquitted in a judgement that cannot, under any plausible interpretation, be squared with the evidence presented at the trial.*[41]

Following the trial, the two military prosecutors in the case took the unprecedented step of submitting a memorandum to the AFP Chief of Staff expressing their belief that "...at least four of the accused should have been found guilty of the offence since six witnesses of the prosecution positively identified them."

The Lupao case was seen as a test of the new government's commitment to protecting human rights and, in particular, to bringing suspected perpetrators to justice. The outcome demonstrated the government's lack of resolve in this respect; it also represented a milestone in the re-emergence of a pattern of impunity in the Philippines.

Mary Concepcion Bautista, Chairman of the Commission on Human Rights (CHR). The CHR was established in May 1987 as an independent government agency to investigate all forms of human rights violations. However, limitations in its mandate, methods of work and personnel, as well as lack of cooperation from police and military authorities, have impeded its effectiveness. The CHR lacks the authority to bring suspected perpetrators to justice and it has often failed to conduct aggressive, thorough investigations of reported human rights violations.

The Commission on Human Rights (CHR)

The *Komisyon ng Karapatang Pantao*, Commission on Human Rights (CHR), was officially established in May 1987 as an independent government agency to investigate "all forms of human rights violations involving civil and political rights". It replaced the Presidential Committee on Human Rights (PCHR), which effectively disbanded in January 1987 following the Mendiola Bridge incident[42]. Members of the CHR are appointed by the President for seven-year terms and confirmation by Congress is not required.

The CHR has proved to be notably ineffective in: (1) providing immediate and effective protection to complainants in human rights cases; and (2) providing remedy, in the longer term, by bringing to account those responsible for gross human rights violations constituting criminal offenses under Philippine law.[43] Its effectiveness has been impeded by certain limitations in its own mandate, methods of work and personnel, and by a lack of full cooperation from the security forces. The CHR also lacks the authority to bring suspected perpetrators to justice. The CHR can only make recommendations for referral of cases to either civil or military prosecutorial agencies, provide modest financial assistance to victims and offer some protection to witnesses.[44]

From the outset the CHR has defined human rights much more broadly than its predecessor, the PCHR. Whereas the PCHR's mandate was limited to violations committed by people acting on behalf of the government, the CHR's mandate covers "all forms of human rights violations". The CHR leadership has interpreted this to include abuses by armed opposition groups such as the NPA and the MNLF, as well as a wide range of criminal acts and civil disputes, including car theft, insurance claims, breaches of contract and marital problems. In doing so, the CHR has developed a concept of human rights which bears little relation to that defined within the terms of the international human rights treaties to which the Philippines is a party. Moreover, the CHR has failed to establish clear priorities in dealing with the thousands of such "violations" reported each year. This has stretched the CHR's already limited resources and has impaired its capacity to deal adequately with pervasive human rights violations by government forces.

Victims and witnesses of human rights violations, human rights lawyers, and even government officials have questioned the thoroughness and impartiality of CHR investigations. In July 1989 the then Undersecretary of Justice said: "The CHR must strengthen its fact-finding capabilities. As it is they can't even investigate a simple case."

Amnesty International's own observations in the field tend to support the conclusion that CHR investigations, with some notable exceptions, are all too often a bureaucratic formality. In the majority of cases CHR officials fail to carry out first-hand investigations, relying instead on information provided by government or military authorities or reports from other organizations. Like other investigative agencies in the Philippines, the CHR places an inordinate burden on complainants and witnesses to provide the evidence necessary for prosecution, in spite of the obvious limitations and dangers inherent in such an approach. Investigations are frequently stopped and cases "archived" at the smallest indication of resistance from the authorities or where a key witness has failed to come forward to testify. Yet it is precisely in these circumstances that the CHR ought to exert its authority, for example, to ensure that witnesses feel free to testify without fear of reprisal.

The CHR has introduced procedures which make complainants and witnesses vulnerable to threats and intimidation without, in general, providing the effective remedy that might ideally be afforded by a court of law. For example, complainants and witnesses must provide public testimony, give their names and addresses, and appear repeatedly before hearings. Partly as a result of these procedures, witnesses and complainants, as well as their relatives and legal counsel, are routinely subjected to harassment, death threats and acts of violence by those suspected of killings or their agents. CHR hearings do not fall within the jurisdiction of the criminal justice system, nor do their findings have legal validity in court proceedings. Those wishing to pursue human rights complaints and to seek judicial remedy must therefore undergo an entirely separate process through which complainants and witnesses must again put their lives at risk.

Another factor limiting the effectiveness of the CHR is the public perception that it lacks independence from the government and the security forces. Several key posts, including Director of Investigations and Director of Information of the CHR, have been held for periods of time by former military officers. There has also been evidence of military infiltration into the CHR.[45] More importantly, the CHR has often appeared to adopt uncritically the position of the government and the military with regard to unlawful killings and other serious human rights violations. For example, the CHR apparently accepted without question the acquittal of soldiers believed responsible for the Lupao massacre, in spite of a substantial body of evidence indicating their guilt. Similarly, a superficial CHR report, dated August 1990, on the torture and killing of nine fishpond workers in Paombong in April 1989 exonerated the 28 suspects, despite eye-witness and other testimony strongly suggesting their guilt. CHR investigations into the rape and killing of two women in Mondragon, Northern Samar, in July 1989, were reportedly stopped by the Chairman after a military officer claimed that the allegations of military responsibility were false. Moreover, as noted in Chapter 3, the Chairman accused the CHR's Samar office of fabricating evidence and an eye-witness of lying about the case.

On the positive side, the CHR's 12 regional offices do provide some protection to victims and their representatives. In remote areas, where local non-governmental human rights organizations are themselves under threat, the CHR often provides the only mechanism through which complaints can be registered and inquiries set in motion. The extent to which the CHR provides protection depends greatly, however, on the personal qualities and commitment of its regional personnel.

Military justice

Amnesty International is aware of no conviction since 1986 for extrajudicial execution of any member of the police or military forces as a consequence of a trial by a military court. Prosecution of those suspected of human rights violations has been impeded by Presidential Decree 1850 (PD 1850), which was in force until June 1991, and by the lack of rigour with which military and police authorities have conducted investigations into alleged human rights violations.

PD 1850 was promulgated by former President Marcos in 1982. It provided for military court jurisdiction in all criminal cases involving military and police defendants, regardless of the nature of the offence committed. Except in isolated instances when the President exercised her right to waive PD 1850, this meant that civil courts had no jurisdiction over cases involving human rights violations committed by members of the security forces. Under both the Marcos and Aquino governments, PD 1850 was used consistently to safeguard soldiers and police officers against legal action following allegations of criminal acts or human rights violations. Amnesty International welcomed the repeal of PD 1850.

It remains to be seen whether cases involving alleged human rights violations by members of the security forces will, in practice, be referred to the civil courts or will continue to be treated as crimes committed in the course of duty and therefore under the jurisdiction of military courts. In this respect, it is encouraging that Republic Act 7055, the law repealing PD 1850, stipulates that the decision about jurisdiction is to be made by a civil court judge. However, if human rights cases remain, in practice, within the jurisdiction of the military courts, the problem of impunity will remain intractable.

One reason is that military prosecutors have consistently failed to pursue cases of alleged human rights violations. As a result the prosecution of suspected human rights offenders before military courts has been extremely rare. When they have taken up such cases, the efforts of military prosecutors have been notably lacking in impartiality and rigour. They have done little to obtain additional evidence, relying heavily on information provided by complainants or witnesses. Nor have they, in general, pursued cases further if for any reason such information is not forthcoming. The UN Working Group on Enforced or Involuntary Disappearance, which visited the Philippines in 1990, observed that:

> *"Unfortunately, the [Working Group] members...did not come away impressed by the modus operandi of the administration of military justice. In view of the overwhelming testimonies on involvement of members of the public forces in cases of...human rights abuses, the number of convictions is surprisingly low."*

Police and military investigations into reported human rights violations have also been characterized by a lack of impartiality and thoroughness. In many cases the authorities have blamed reported killings on the NPA despite lack of evidence to support such allegations. In other cases, they have stated that their investigations were facing a "blank wall", even though there were important leads yet to be pursued. Suspects have been identified and charged only in a few exceptional cases following strong intervention by civilian officials or agencies such as the National Bureau of Investigation, the Department of Justice or, on occasion, the CHR. Even where a suspect is identified and charged, the police often refuse or fail to serve the warrant for arrest, allowing the suspect to remain at large.

Military and police authorities have attempted to justify the failure to conduct proper investigations into killings, or to bring the perpetrators to justice, by claiming that they took place during an armed encounter during which rebels were shot, or that civilians were caught in cross-fire. When non-governmental organizations, the church or the media have presented clear evidence of military involvement in unlawful executions, those responsible have offered *ex-gratia* financial payments to the relatives of the victims.

But they have not taken action to identify and bring to justice the perpetrators of the killings. The reliance on such "amicable settlements" of serious human rights violations reflects a generalized failure of the judicial system, which in turn perpetuates the pattern of abuse.

Virtually all security force agencies with investigative responsibilities — including the INP, the National Police Commission (NAPOLCOM), the Inspectorate of the AFP, and the Provost Martial — have suffered similar shortcomings. They are often responsible for investigating charges against members of their own unit or officers of a higher rank. As a rule they are unenthusiastic about pursuing such investigations. This problem has been exacerbated by the fact that under the current government several military officers, both retired and active, have been appointed to key positions in agencies with some responsibility for investigation into alleged police and military abuses. They include the current Director of the NBI, the Secretary of the Interior and Local Government, the Secretary of National Defense, the Director of the PNP and several commissioners and staff members of the CHR.

The Secretary of National Defense and the Chief of Staff of the Armed Forces have taken a series of initiatives since 1986 aimed, ostensibly, at improving the monitoring and investigation of human rights violations. However, available evidence suggests that these initiatives, like many of the investigations themselves, have been intended primarily to improve the image of the armed forces rather than to punish the offenders or put an end to human rights violations.

Following the change of government in 1986 "Special Action Committees" were established in each AFP Area Command to deal with reports of human rights violations. By the end of 1988 these committees had received 133 complaints. Of these, 36 were dismissed "due to lack of merit", 51 were "awaiting investigation results" and 46 were under "ongoing investigation". None had resulted in convictions. Since late 1988, the Department of National Defense has provided no further information on the work of the committees.

In 1989 the Department of National Defense established a Human Rights Division. This was intended to monitor human rights cases and to liaise with governmental and non-governmental organizations. The Division appears to have devoted most of its efforts to cleansing the human rights image of the armed forces, and rather little to the substantive investigation of human rights violations. As noted earlier, the Department of National Defense has not responded to specific requests for information by Amnesty International concerning alleged human rights violations and the prosecution of suspected offenders.

Investigations have occasionally been initiated at the national level by military authorities following inquiries or appeals by Amnesty International. In a few instances these appear to have resulted in instructions or advisory notices from the central command to Area or Provincial Commanders concerning the alleged violations. In at least one such case, however, the military investigation conducted was neither thorough nor impartial. In his July 1990 report to the Secretary of National Defense, the Commander of the AFP Southern Command dismissed reports of death threats against human rights lawyer, Solema Jubilan, and Amnesty International's expression of concern about these threats, as leftist "propaganda". The report also gave credence to unproven allegations that Attorney Jubilan's orphanage in Kidapawan was "a front of the NPA/CPP in their fund-raising activities". Moreover, he implied that Amnesty International was actively involved in the alleged unlawful activities.

In response to some of the most highly publicized instances of human rights violations, military commanders have periodically appointed internal *ad-hoc* fact-finding teams to conduct investigations. Such investigations were carried out into the killing of two people during a funeral procession in Metro Manila in June 1990; the extrajudicial execution of 19 members of a family in Sultan Kudarat in August 1990; and the massacre of nine people at Paombong, Bulacan in April 1989. In spite of substantial evidence of armed forces responsibility, these investigations either cleared the suspects or led to an acquittal in a military court trial.

Prosecution in the civil courts

The civilian courts have had only a marginally better record than military courts with respect to convictions for human rights violations. Their power to prosecute has been limited, of course, by PD 1850. Yet, even where civilian courts have heard human rights cases, the record of conviction has not been impressive. Effective prosecution has been undermined by several factors, including the fear of witnesses to testify; the lack of autonomy of prosecutors and judges; obstruction and lack of cooperation by police and military officials; and the judicial norms which place the burden of proof on the complainant. Civil courts, including the Supreme Court, have also been ineffective in helping to relocate those reported to have "disappeared", thereby increasing the risk of their becoming the victims of extrajudicial execution or torture.

Members of the security forces suspected of responsibility for extrajudicial executions or other human rights violations have frequently avoided prosecution through intimidation or harassment of the victim's relatives and witnesses. Intimidation has included death threats and has sometimes resulted in the killing of witnesses, relatives and defence lawyers. These dangers have done much to hamper the effective prosecution of suspected perpetrators of unlawful killings.

Lawyers, prosecutors and judges involved in human rights related cases have also been intimidated by members of government and government-backed forces. A disturbing number of lawyers have been killed, including at least seven human rights lawyers, since 1986. Police and military authorities have also threatened to bring criminal charges against human rights lawyers.[46] Observers at court hearings in human rights and political cases have noted the presence of heavily armed men in military and civilian clothes in the courtroom and in the immediate vicinity. In this environment it has been difficult for judges and prosecutors to remain independent. Filipino jurists consider judges who dare to "clip the wings" of the military or police, by ruling against them in human rights or political cases, to be "rare and brave".

Civil prosecutors have not been centrally involved in human rights cases against members of the security forces, principally because of PD 1850. Yet, even in cases where the jurisdiction of military courts has been waived, prosecutors have been reluctant to pursue such cases unless the victims, relatives or witnesses are willing to gather the evidence. Successful prosecution has also been prevented by the refusal of military or police officials to cooperate with the prosecutorial agencies. The forms of non-cooperation have included withholding evidence and military records, refusing access to military personnel or installations and transferring military suspects to a different part of the country.

Effective prosecution of human rights cases in the civil courts has also been impeded by certain judicial norms. For example, the judiciary has tended to accept without hesitation the statements of law enforcement agencies, while dismissing the testimony of witnesses as insufficient proof of culpability. The courts have often failed to challenge the statements of law enforcement and military officials that are at odds with the body of independent testimonial and material evidence. Several Filipino jurists have attributed this court practice to a principle described as the "presumption of regularity" in official procedures and institutions. A presumption of regularity in a context in which extralegal and covert acts have become a normal part of security force operations, serves as a significant constraint on the use of legal remedies to bring to justice those responsible for arbitrary killings.

The pursuit of legal remedy in the case of "disappearance" is also ineffective. *Habeas corpus* petitions have rarely been effective as a method of locating persons last seen in police or military custody. In general, the courts have failed to act promptly to determine the whereabouts and legal status of unacknowledged detainees who are the subject of habeas corpus petitions, or to rule firmly against military respondents in such cases. Delays of several months in the resolution of such cases are common. In one recent case a *habeas corpus* proceeding lasted for more than a year without effective resolution.

Recent Supreme Court rulings have given more power to the security forces to arrest suspected political opponents without a warrant. This has further undermined the remedy of *habeas corpus* and may increase the risk of the "disappearance" and extrajudicial execution of political detainees. The Supreme Court decision of 9 July 1990 (Umil v. Ramos, GR No. 81567) for example, ruled that any person may be arrested without a court order if he or she is suspected of rebellion or subversion. The ruling is based on an argument that these crimes are "continuing offenses", that those suspected of these crimes are therefore always in *flagrante delicto* and are consequently subject to arrest without warrant at any time. Where virtually any arrest of a suspected political opponent may be considered legal by the Supreme Court, important legal and constitutional safeguards against arbitrary arrest, "disappearance" and extrajudicial execution are rendered ineffective. In this situation members of the security forces will inevitably feel free to commit unlawful acts with impunity.

Intimidation of witnesses

Witnesses frequently fail to testify against military or police authorities because of a well-founded fear of physical or legal retaliation by the authorities. The intimidation of witnesses and complainants is of particular concern because it pervades virtually every stage of the investigation and prosecution process. It also leads, on occasion; to further unlawful killings.

Almost without exception, government agencies and military authorities explain the absence of successful prosecutions as the consequence of witnesses' "unwillingness" to testify. This is an unsatisfactory explanation. Government and military authorities have a clear obligation to protect witnesses so that they are not afraid to testify for fear of retribution. Until such protection is offered to witnesses there can be no grounds for ending an investigation, or acquitting a suspect.[47]

The Witness Protection Act of April 1991 appears to be a step in the right direction. It provides for protection and assistance to witnesses in serious criminal cases, such as grave felony, *coups d'etat* and murder. In September 1991 the Secretary of Justice announced that witnesses in a number of murder cases would become the first beneficiaries of the program. However, some human rights advocates in the Philippines believe that the act, which is designed primarily to provide material assistance to witnesses, may not provide effective protection from violence or intimidation.[48] An existing measure for the protection of witnesses, counsel and judges in human rights cases is contained in the 1987 Constitution. Article VIII, Section 5(4) provides the Supreme Court with the authority to "order a change of venue or place of trial to avoid a miscarriage of justice". However, this provision has not provided a practical or effective solution to the problem of intimidation of witnesses.[49]

Amnesty International believes that, in addition to an effective witness protection program, other practical measures could be taken to ensure that witnesses can testify without fear of retribution. The government's investigative and prosecutorial agencies should play a more aggressive role in obtaining evidence in human rights related cases, rather than relying on information offered by witnesses and complainants. It should also ensure that those suspected of committing extrajudicial executions or other serious violations are immediately disarmed and removed from positions of authority, pending the results of investigations.

6

The Philippine Government and human rights

The government's human rights initiatives

On taking office President Aquino immediately took important steps aimed at protecting and promoting human rights. She ordered the release of political prisoners, repealed repressive decrees allowing indefinite detention without trial, and restored the right of habeas corpus. A new Constitution, containing important human rights guarantees, was drafted by a commission and ratified by national referendum on 2 February 1987.[50]

After 1986 human rights education was included as a regular part of police and military training. In the same year the government promised to respect several important interna-

This cartoon appeared in a Philippine newspaper in July 1991 following publication of *Amnesty International Report 1991*. ***The exclamation reads: "How exaggerated!"***

tional human rights treaties including the International Covenant on Civil and Political Rights (ICCPR), and the Convention against Torture and Other Cruel, Inhuman or Degrading Treatment or Punishment.[51] In August 1989 the government ratified the First Optional Protocol to the ICCPR. It then invited both the UN Working Group on Enforced or Involuntary Disappearances and the UN Special Rapporteur on Torture to visit the Philippines in 1990, and their reports were made public in early 1991.

Unfortunately, as has been shown, the human rights initiatives have been hampered by an evident lack of commitment to implement them properly.A similar lack of resolve has been evident in implementing human rights initiatives within the armed forces. In February 1989 the Secretary of National Defense announced that respect for human rights would be considered as one of the grounds for officer promotion — a principle reiterated by the President in a guideline issued in July 1991. To Amnesty International's knowledge, this policy has not been actively or consistently pursued. On the contrary, some military officers believed to be responsible for human rights violations have been promoted, and some have been given important executive positions in the government.

In June 1989 the Secretary of National Defense set out the terms of a "clean-up" process to rid the AFP of "undesirable elements". The directive stipulated that officers should be held accountable for the conduct of those under their command; soldiers facing charges before a civil court should be discharged from military service; military authorities should cooperate with the prosecuting authorities in cases of soldiers charged with grave offences and ensure that such soldiers appear before the courts; and firearms should be confiscated from soldiers facing trial. However, these commendable initiatives have had little real impact because they have not been systematically or vigorously implemented.

The government has launched several other human rights initiatives in the past two years. It remains to be seen, however, whether these will be sustained in practice. A Presidential Human Rights Committee (PHRC) was established in December 1988 to "monitor the human rights situation in the country and to advise [the President] on the proper measures to be taken". Though largely inactive in 1989 the PHRC appears recently to have contributed to discussions about human rights issues by members of the government, military authorities and national human rights organizations. It has also coordinated investigations into particular cases of alleged human rights violations, and has been instrumental in drafting guidelines and agreements which governmental and some non-governmental bodies have signed.

One such memorandum of agreement — concerning procedures for the release of detainees, signed in June 1991 — may have particular significance for the future protection of possible victims of extrajudicial execution and "disappearance".[52] The memorandum specifies that the release of individuals from custody must be witnessed by family members, a lawyer engaged by them or appointed by the courts, or a CHR representative. It requires prison officials and security force commanders to maintain an official logbook, which must be open for inspection by any interested party, recording precise details of all detentions and releases. It also stipulates that if a person detained by the security forces subsequently "disappears" or is found dead, the captors must prove that the person was released safely and that proper existing procedures were followed. If they have failed to observe the procedures, the captors and their commanding officers shall be liable for administrative or penal sanctions as provided by law.

In January 1991 the PC and the Integrated National Police (INP) were incorporated into a single new force, the Philippine National Police (PNP). The PNP was placed formally under the authority of the Department of the Interior and Local Government. Amnesty International welcomed this move to restore a measure of civilian control over the security forces. It also welcomed the statement of a PNP officer in July 1991 which said that the Director "will impose drastic action on PNP officers and men who will be found guilty of total disregard for human rights." Amnesty International notes, however, that for the foreseeable future the PNP will continue to play a leading role in the government's counter-insurgency campaign. It will do so under the operational command of the Armed Forces of the Philippines for a minimum of two years. Thereafter it is expected to assume full responsibility for counter-insurgency operations. In the words of one military officer: "The PC is no longer under the military but will remain under military direction when it comes to the counter-insurgency campaign." It is therefore doubtful that, in the absence of more fundamental changes, nominal civilian control of the PNP will have any real impact on the human rights record of the PNP.

Amnesty International has welcomed the Philippine Government's ratification of major international human rights treaties, and other steps it has taken to protect and promote human rights, including the repeal of PD 1850. It emphasizes, however, that international and domestic law oblige the government to provide effective human rights protection, not only in principle but also in practice. Unfortunately, the government's stated intentions have not always been systematically and vigorously implemented in practice.

Amnesty International and the Philippine Government

Amnesty International representatives have visited the Philippines six times since 1986. The first three visits took place between May 1986 and July 1987. In June 1988, during a fact-finding visit, interviews were conducted with government officials, military officers, members of human rights groups, and victims of human rights violations and their relatives. In July 1988 the Secretary General of Amnesty International met President Aquino, the Secretary of National Defense and other members of the government, as well as senior members of the Armed Forces. In April and May 1990 Amnesty International representatives again visited the Philippines on a fact-finding mission. They met CHR officials, military officers, representatives of national human rights organizations, and the victims and witnesses of human rights violations throughout the country.

In the period immediately after the fall of President Marcos, the new government willingly discussed substantive human rights issues with Amnesty International representatives. However, following the publication of a number of reports which expressed serious concern over continuing human rights violations in the Philippines, the government became increasingly critical of Amnesty International. After the release in 1988 of a major report on political killings in the Philippines, the Chairman of the CHR stated that she had notified the President that the report was "one-sided and therefore unacceptable".

In recent years, other government representatives, including the President, have suggested that the organization's reports are exaggerated or based on inaccurate or politically biased information. In a statement to the media in July 1989, the President said that Amnesty International reported "non-existing human rights violations" and that its claims were "without basis". The government has also alleged that the organization does not seek the government's views on the human rights situation in the Philippines or reflect these in its published documents. In a letter to a local newspaper on 7 February 1990, the Chairman of the CHR claimed that various human rights organizations, including Amnesty International:

> *"...had been challenged and invited in vain by the [CHR] to substantiate all their extravagant propaganda statements with documents, names of victims and produce witnesses to these human rights violations and they have miserably failed to do so...These groups, like the leftist propagandists abroad, have campaigned in vain against the Philippines..."*

In fact, since mid-1988 copies of every document published by Amnesty International and copies of every substantive letter to government and military authorities have been submitted to the government or the CHR for comment. Every major publication has outlined the government's human rights initiatives. Where there has been a substantive government response to an Amnesty International report, this has been reflected in subsequent reports.

In May 1991, in preparation for this report, Amnesty International's Secretary General wrote to the Secretary of National Defense requesting information on more than 100 cases of alleged extrajudicial execution, and details of the cases of security force members whom the government claimed had been prosecuted and sentenced for unlawful killings. By November 1991, Amnesty International had not received a reply. A similar letter written to the CHR was answered but the response provided information on only three of the 105 cases of extrajudicial execution referred to by Amnesty International.[53]

Several other letters from Amnesty International to the Department of National Defense and the President requesting information about apparent extrajudicial executions have also gone unanswered. In July 1990 Amnesty International wrote to President Aquino about the deliberate killing of two people by members of the security forces at a funeral procession in Manila on 28 June 1990. In a letter of 7 September 1990, Amnesty International welcomed the decision of the Secretary of National Defense to initiate an investigation into the killing of 19 members of a family in Sultan Kudarat on 3 August 1990, and asked to be kept informed of the results. In February 1991 Amnesty International wrote to request the comments of the Department of National Defense on an Amnesty International report on "disappearances" in the Philippines.

In March 1991 Amnesty International wrote to the Secretary of National Defense requesting his comments on an Amnesty International report about the extrajudicial execution of Father Narciso Pico in January 1991. Unfortunately, as of November 1991, Amnesty International had not received replies to any of these letters.

On the positive side, some government agencies have recently begun to provide substantive replies to Amnesty International's queries and reports. Both the Department of Labor and Employment and the CHR provided detailed responses to a report on human rights violations against trade unionists published by Amnesty International in June 1991.[54] The organization has also received a substantial number of detailed replies on specific cases as well as broader legal issues from the Department of Justice. While the replies are not, in Amnesty International's view, always complete and do not in themselves provide any guarantee that human rights violations will be prevented, they are unquestionably a sign of the government's renewed willingness to engage in a dialogue about substantive human rights concerns. It is in the hope of maintaining the momentum of this dialogue that the current report is written, and the following recommendations are made.

7

Amnesty International's proposals to stop the killings

Amnesty International believes that the following recommendations, if implemented, would strengthen existing human rights guarantees in the Philippines, and would in particular help to prevent future extrajudicial executions. Many of these recommendations are based on the *Principles on the Effective Prevention and Investigation of Extra-legal, Arbitrary and Summary Executions*, which were endorsed by the UN General Assembly in December 1989.

To create a political climate in which extrajudicial executions are less likely to occur, Amnesty International urges the government to:

1. Issue clear and unequivocal orders that the counter-insurgency campaign must be carried out within the framework of national and international law, and that violations of human rights will not be tolerated under any circumstances;
2. Ensure strict control, including a clear chain of command, over all officials authorized to use force and firearms, as well as officials responsible for arrest, detention or imprisonment;
3. Ensure that any member of the security forces or government who is suspected of ordering, inciting, suggesting, encouraging or facilitating extrajudicial executions is immediately discharged from his or her duties and investigated;
4. Ensure that Constitutional provisions prohibiting the maintenance of private armies and paramilitary groups are upheld and enforced by dismantling all armed vigilante groups and adopting legislation explicitly prohibiting their operation;

5. Take immediate measures to ensure that only those fully authorized to use force and bear arms are permitted to do so; and in particular to ensure that arms are not provided to vigilantes and other unofficial groups;
6. Disband the CAFGUs as soon as possible and in the meantime ensure that all militia units are immediately brought under effective control by military authorities;
7. Prohibit explicitly the public "red-labelling" of alleged government opponents by government authorities and by members of government and government-backed security forces.

To ensure that extrajudicial executions cannot be committed with impunity, Amnesty International calls on the government to:

8. Initiate prompt, thorough and impartial investigations into all reports of unlawful killing by members of government and government-backed forces;
9. Bring promptly to justice before a civil court all members of government and government-backed security forces suspected of responsibility for extrajudicial executions and related crimes such as issuing death threats;
10. Ensure that members of the security forces implicated in extrajudicial executions or related crimes are immediately disarmed and removed from positions of power or control, whether direct or indirect, over complainants, witnesses and their relatives, investigators and lawyers;
11. Ensure that the various investigative and prosecutorial agencies actively and systematically pursue all reports of human rights violations. Responsibility for the task of obtaining evidence and bringing criminal charges against suspects must be fully assumed by the authorities, and not left to complainants or witnesses;
12. Establish a practical and affordable witness protection program, which would strengthen the existing program, and ensure that complainants, witnesses and investigators in human rights-related cases are protected from violence, threats of violence or any other form of intimidation;
13. Undertake a thorough review of the Commission on Human Rights, its terms of reference, procedures and methods of work.

14. Continue to cooperate fully with international bodies investigating extrajudicial executions and invite the UN Special Rapporteur on Summary or Arbitrary Executions to visit the Philippines.

To ensure that detention procedures provide guarantees against the extrajudicial execution (death in custody) of detainees and prisoners, Amnesty International calls on the government to:

15. Guarantee that judicial and quasi-judicial bodies shall be granted access to all places of detention where a detainee is suspected of being held;

16. Enforce the legal and constitutional prohibition of incommunicado detention or the use of unofficial places of detention;

FOOTNOTES

Introduction

[1] A major report *Unlawful Killings by Military and Paramilitary Forces* was published by Amnesty International in March 1988 (ASA 35/02/88). Since then, reports on political killings have included: *Extrajudicial Executions and "Disappearances" in Manila*, May 1988 (ASA 35/08/88), *The Killing and Intimidation of Human Rights Lawyers*, August 1988 (ASA 35/25/88), *Extrajudicial Executions and Torture of Trade Unionists*, March 1989 (ASA 35/03/89), *The Killing of Narciso Pico, A Parish Priest*, March 1991 (ASA 35/08/91), *Human Rights Violations and the Labour Movement*, June 1991 (ASA 35/16/91).

[2] Amnesty International has published a number of reports on "disappearance" in the Philippines. These include: *Philippines: "Disappearances" since June 1988*, April 1989 (ASA 35/09/89) and *Philippines: "Disappearances" in a Context of Counter-insurgency*, February 1991 (ASA 35/05/91).The torture of those held in custody in the Philippines has been documented in a number of Amnesty International reports, including *Philippines: Incommunicado Detention*, Ill-treatment and Torture during 1988, December 1988 (ASA 35/40/88).

[3] These violations have been documented in a number of Amnesty International Reports including: *Philippines: The Imprisonment of Farmers from Leyte*, October 1988 (ASA 35/34/88); *Philippines: Case Studies in the Use of the Death Penalty*, April 1989 (ASA 35/08/89); *Philippines: Imprisonment of Peasant Leader - Jaime Tadeo*, June 1990 (ASA 35/17/90); *Philippines: A Summary of Amnesty* International's Concerns, March 1990 (ASA 35/02/90).

Chapter 1

[4] The United Nations Special Rapporteur on Summary or Arbitrary Executions has described the right to life as: *"...the most important and basic of human rights. It is the fountain from which all human rights spring. If it is infringed the effects are irreversible..."* UN Doc.ECN.4/1983/16, Paragraph 22.

[5] On 21 February 1989, the Philippine Representative to the UN Commission on Human Rights declared: "No human rights violations will be tolerated or go unpunished". He quoted Section 11, Article II of the Constitution which states: "The State values the dignity of every human person and guarantees full respect for human rights."

[6] Section 1 of the Bill of Rights states that: *"No person shall be deprived of life, liberty, or property without due process of law, nor shall any person be denied the equal protection of the laws."* See Appendix I for excerpts from the Bill of Rights relating to human rights.

[7] The Philippine Government acceded to the Geneva Conventions on 6 October 1952.

Chapter 2

[8] Amnesty International published two major reports concerning human rights violations under the government of President Marcos: *Report of an Amnesty International Mission to the Republic of the Philippines, 22 November - 2 December 1975*, was published in July 1976; *Report of an Amnesty International Mission to*

the Republic of the Philippines, 11 - 22 November 1981, was published in August 1982.

[9] Mindanao has a population of about 12 million, about one third of which is Muslim. Collectively referred to as the Moro, the Muslim population is divided among 11 smaller ethno-linguistic groups.

[10] In 1990, the government estimated the combined strength of all armed Muslim opposition groups at about 21,500.

[11] EDSA stands for Epifanio de los Santos Avenue, the highway which crosses Manila, upon which Camps Aguinaldo and Crame (the Army and Philippine Constabulary headquarters respectively) are situated.

[12] The campaign is sometimes referred to in the Philippines as the "total war" policy or approach.

[13] A senior military commander responsible for operations described the change in military strategy as follows: "...instead of conventional operations against the NPA main force units, the AFP would break its battalions into squads to attack the communist mass base...".

[14] Testifying before the Senate Committee on Justice and Human Rights in May 1989, two military officers complained that "...the burden of being denounced for human rights violations threatens the effectiveness of the military because it diminishes the soldier's will to fight".

[15] A fourth "development" phase is aimed at bringing about long term socio-economic changes in order to undercut support for the insurgency.

[16] The Department of Social Welfare and Development has estimated the number of people affected by forced evacuations as follows: January to September 1988 - 192,443; 1989 - 221,302; January to June 1990 - 139,278. Independent organizations such as the Ecumenical Movement for Justice and Peace and Task Force Detainees, give slightly higher figures. Forced evacuations also occurred under the government of President Marcos. From 1972 to 1984, more than one million people were estimated to have evacuated their homes as a result of military operations.

Chapter 3

[17] See Appendix II for the text of a letter from Amnesty International to the Secretary of National Defense in May 1991. A similar letter was sent to the CHR. The CHR's response is reproduced in Appendix III.

[18] See *Philippines: A Summary of Amnesty International's Concerns*, February 1991 (ASA 35/02/90)

[19] See Appendix II for the text of Amnesty International's 1 May 1991 letter to the Secretary of National Defense. A similar letter was sent to the CHR. See Appendix III for the text of CHR Chairman's reply to Amnesty International of 29 May 1991.

[20] See *Philippines: "Disappearances" in a Context of Counter-insurgency*, February 1991 (ASA 35/05/91).

[21] Hundreds of trade unionists and members of peasant and farmers' organizations have been arrested over the past five years in the Philippines. Dozens have been charged with crimes such as inciting to sedition, illegal association, subversion, rebellion, illegal possession of firearms and illegal assembly. Amnesty International

believes that some might be prisoners of conscience if they were imprisoned on the charges they face.

[22] The torture was alleged to have included electric shocks and "water cure", a method of torture which involves the near suffocation of the victim with water.

[23] Human rights violations against trade unionists, including details of 11 incidents of apparent extrajudicial execution, were documented in detail in the Amnesty International report: *Philippines: Human Rights Violations and the Labour Movement*, June 1991 (ASA 35/16/91). The report included details of seven NFSW members believed to have been killed by government or government-backed forces.

[24] Amnesty International issued an urgent appeal on behalf of church workers who had received death threats in June 1989 *Philippines: 25 People Named on Hit Lists*, 26 June 1989 ASA 35/21/89); see also *Philippines: Sister Aquila Sy*, 11 September 1990 (ASA 35/23/91).

[25] The murder of Narciso Pico was first documented by Amnesty International in *Philippines: The Killing of Parish Priest, Narciso Pico*, March 1991 (ASA 35/08/91).

[26] "Rebel-returnees" are known to be used extensively by the military as informers on NPA activity and membership. They are believed to be subjected to pressure to comply with military demands for information. In some cases their physical safety may depend upon continued denunciations of both real and suspected members of the NPA.

[27] For further information see *Philippines: The Killing and Intimidation of Human Rights Lawyers* August 1988 (ASA 35/25/88).

[28] For further information see *Philippines: Alfonso Surigao*, 27 June 1988 (ASA 35/12/88).

[29] One of the detainees was released on bail in mid-1988. She and 12 others were acquitted and the 12 were released on 10 May 1990. Another prisoner was released on bail in December 1990. The remaining 12 remain in detention, pending a final verdict by the courts. For further information see the Amnesty International report *Philippines: The Imprisonment of Farmers from Leyte*, October 1988 (ASA 35/34/88).

[30] "Military assets" may be surrendered or captured members of the armed opposition or members or unofficial paramilitary groups. They provide the military with information about alleged "subversives" and sometimes carry out political killings.

[31] "Technical arrest" means that the suspect is obliged to remain at a named military detachment and at the disposal of the officers investigating the case in which he or she is involved. The suspect is placed under no other restrictions, however, and is free to move around within the military camp.

[32] For further information see Philippines: The Killing of Human Rights Lawyer Oscar Tonog, April 1989 (ASA 35/10/89).

[33] See Appendix II for the text of Amnesty International's May 1991 letter to the Department of National Defense.

Chapter 4

[34] Estimates of the numbers of those killed vary considerably. Some former NPA members have alleged that as many as 200 were killed and military spokesmen have quoted figures of "more than 100".

Chapter 5

[35] In an exceptional case, 16 military men were convicted by a government corruption court in September 1990, for the 1983 murder of former Senator Benigno Aquino, the President's late husband.

[36] In one copy of the list made available to a human rights organization, the ranks of the three had been crudely deleted, apparently to create the impression that they had been civilian victims of extrajudicial execution. Another copy of the same list, received by Amnesty International, indicated their ranks clearly.

[37] Sergeant Mar[c]iano Contaoe, a member of the Presidential Security Group, was sentenced to 300 years in prison for the murder of nine people while he was in a drunken rage near his home in Taguig, Manila on 21 May 1988. According to press reports, he "ran amok" after his drinking partners taunted him about the military's failure to control crime in the neighbourhood.

[38] Excerpts from The Department of Labor and Employment's 14-page response are reproduced in Appendix IV.

[39] See Appendix II for the text of Amnesty International's 1 May 1991 letters to the Department of National Defense. See Appendix III for the CHR's response of 29 May 1991.

[40] For details of the Lupao massacre, see Amnesty International's report, *Philippines: Unlawful Killings by Military and Paramilitary Forces*, March 1988 (ASA 35/02/88).

[41] Lawyers Committee for Human Rights, *Impunity: Prosecutions of Human Rights Violations in the Philippines*, September 1991.

[42] On 22 January 1987, government troops opened fire on members of a peasant organization during a demonstration at Mendiola Bridge in Manila. Thirteen people were killed during the incident.

[43] According to the CHR, only 70 cases of alleged human rights violations by military personnel between 1986 and December 1988 "merited further investigation and referral to the AFP". Of these, three were dismissed for lack of evidence, three resulted in the discharge of the military personnel, 14 were to be heard by a court martial, three were referred to civilian courts and 47 were under pre-trial investigation. Of 504 cases investigated by the CHR in 1989, 325 were "terminated with draft resolutions and 179 were otherwise "resolved". Of the 179 "resolved" cases, 72 had been "terminated" and 23 "archived". The remaining 84 cases were filed with various prosecutorial agencies. As of May 1990, the CHR reported that a judgment had been rendered in 53 cases. Forty-one of these resulted in acquittal or dismissal of charges, and only four resulted in conviction.

[44] While PD 1850 was still in effect, the CHR also had authority to recommend to the President that military jurisdiction be waived in specific cases.

[45] On 31 July 1989, 35-year-old Modesto Pasana, a former political detainee, was arrested without warrant in Quezon City and taken to a military camp. He was

interrogated and threatened with death by an officer who was later discovered to be simultaneously employed by the CHR and the PC Capital Regional Command (CAPCOM). On 9 August Modesto Pasana filed charges against the CHR officer, alleging grave threats. In January and February 1990 he was visited by another CHR investigator, who reportedly pressed him to withdraw these charges. In March 1990 the CHR reported that the CAPCOM officer had been discharged from service in November 1989.

[46] For further information on the killing and intimidation of human rights lawyers see, for example: *Philippines: The Killing and Intimidation of Human Rights Lawyers*, August 19988 (ASA 35/25/88); *The Philippines: The Killing of Human Rights Lawyer Oscar Tonog* (ASA 25/10/89); *Death Threats: Attorney Solema P Jubilan*, (ASA 35/16/90), *Death Threats: Attorney Nerio Zamora*, 14 January 1991 and 5 June 1991 (ASA 35/01/91, ASA 35/18/91); *Death Threats: Attorney Wilfred D Asis*, 27 September 1991 (ASA 35/30/91)

[47] Principle 15 of the *UN Principles on the Effective Prevention and Investigation of Extra-legal, Arbitrary and Summary Executions* specifies, in part, that "complainants, witnesses, those conducting the investigation and their families shall be protected from violence, threats of violence or any other form of intimidation".

[48] The benefits provided to witnesses under the act include: free housing before, during and after testifying if the threat to life still exists; job assistance; reasonable travelling and subsistence expenses; and in the case of death, burial benefits and free education for the victim's heirs.

[49] It was invoked at the request of lawyers acting on behalf of 26 farmers from Leyte province, adopted by Amnesty International as prisoners of conscience. Their trial was held in Cebu, rather than Leyte, because the prisoners were afraid of revenge attacks by local vigilantes. Despite the change of venue, security forces were widely believed to have been involved in the assassination of Dr Nemesio Prudente President of the Polytechnic University of the Philippines (PUP), who had assisted the group, and of Attorney Alfonso Surigao, who was representing the defendants in Cebu.

Chapter 6

[50] See Appendix I for excerpts from the Bill of Rights of the 1987 Constitution.

[51] The government ratified the ICCPR in February 1986 and it was deposited with the Office of the UN Secretary General on 23 October 1986. The treaty entered into force in the Philippines on 23 January 1987. In March and April 1989 the Philippines Government reported to the Human Rights Committee, in accordance with its obligations as a state party to the ICCPR. The government acceded to the Convention Against Torture in June 1986.

[52] Signatories to the Memorandum included the Secretaries of the Department of National Defense, the Department of Justice and the Department of Interior and Local Government, the Chief of Staff of the AFP, the Director General of the PNP and the Chairman of the CHR. The full text of the memorandum is reproduced in Appendix V.

[53] The text of Amnesty International's letter to the Secretary of National Defense is reproduced in Appendix II. The CHR's response to a similar letter is reproduced in Appendix III.

[54] See Appendix IV for excerpts from the Department of Labor and Employment's July 1991 response to Amnesty International. The CHR has provided information about a number of individual cases and this has been incorportated, where relevant, into the text of this report.

APPENDIX I

Excerpts from the 1987 Constitution of the Philippines

Article III - The Bill of Rights

Section 1
No person shall be deprived of life, liberty, or property without due process of law, nor shall any person be denied the equal protection of the laws.

Section 2
The right of the people to be secure in their persons, houses, papers, and effects against unreasonable searches and seizures of whatever nature and for any purpose shall be inviolable, and no search warrant or warrant of arrest shall issue except upon probable cause to be determined personally by the judge after examination under oath or affirmation of the complainant and the witnesses he may produce, and particularly describing the place to be searched and the persons or things to be seized.

Section 4
No law shall be passed abridging the freedom of speech, of expression, or of the press, or the right of the people peaceably to assemble and petition the government for redress of grievances.

Section 11
Free access to the courts and quasi-judicial bodies and adequate legal assistance shall not be denied to any person by reason of poverty.

Section 12
(1) Any person under investigation for the commission of an offense shall have theright to be informed of his right to remain silent and to have competent and independent counsel preferably of his own choice. If the person cannot afford the services of counsel, he must be provided with one. These rights cannot be waived except in writing and in the presence of counsel.

(2) No torture, force, violence, threat, intimidation, or any other means which vitiate the free will shall be used against him. Secret detention places, solitary, incommunicado, or other similar forms of detention are prohibited.

(3) Any confession or admission obtained in violation of this or Section 17 hereof shall be inadmissible in evidence against him.

(4) The law shall provide for penal and civil sanctions for violations of this sectionas well as compensation to and rehabilitation of victims of torture or similarpractices, and their families.

Section 15
The privilege of the writ of habeas corpus shall not be suspended except in cases of invasion or rebellion when the public safety requires it.

Section 16
All persons shall have the right to a speedy disposition of their cases before all judicial, quasi-judicial, or administrative bodies.

Section 18

(1) No person shall be detained solely by reason of his political beliefs and aspirations.

Section 19

(1) Excessive fines shall not be imposed, nor cruel, degrading or inhuman punishment inflicted. Neither shall death penalty be imposed, unless, for compelling reasons involving heinous crimes, the Congress hereafter provides for it. Any death penalty already imposed shall be reduced to *reclusion perpetua*.

(2) The employment of physical, psychological, or degrading punishment against any prisoner or detainee or the use of substandard or inadequate penal facilities under subhuman conditions shall be dealt with by law.

APPENDIX II

Text of Amnesty International's 1 May 1991 letter to the Secretary of National Defense. A similar letter was sent on the same day to the Chairman of the CHR.

Also reproduced here is a list of more than 200 people believed to have been killed by government or government-backed forces between 1988 and 1991, which was sent with the letters.

amnesty international

INTERNATIONAL SECRETARIAT,
1 Easton Street, London WC1X 8DJ,
United Kingdom.

Ref.: TG ASA 35/91.06

General Fidel V. Ramos
Secretary of National Defense
Department of National Defense
Camp General Aguinaldo
Quezon City
The Philippines

1 May 1991

Dear General Ramos,

I am writing to express Amnesty International's concern about the considerable number of extrajudicial executions reportedly committed by government and government-backed troops since 1988, and to ask for your assistance in obtaining detailed information on the initiatives taken by the government and the Armed Forces of the Philippines (AFP) to investigate these killings and to bring the perpetrators to justice.

Over the past three years Amnesty International has received reports of more than 300 apparent extrajudicial executions by members of government and government-backed security forces in the Philippines. Some of those killed have been members of lawful non-governmental organizations alleged by government and military authorities to be fronts for the NPA and the CPP. Others have been suspected NPA/CPP members or sympathizers or simply people living in areas of suspected rebel activity. In all of the cases of concern to Amnesty International, the victims were reportedly unarmed and were said to have been deliberately killed by security forces, sometimes while in their custody.

Amnesty International has written to you and other members of the government on several occasions during the last three years seeking clarification of the circumstances of such killings, urging the initiation of prompt and impartial inquiries and asking to be kept informed about the outcome of any official investigations. In July 1990 I wrote to President Aquino concerning the deliberate killing of two people by elements of the security forces during a funeral procession on 28 June in Manila. In a letter of 7 September 1990, Amnesty International welcomed your decision to initiate an investigation into the killing of 19 members of a family in Sultan Kudarat province on 3 August 1990, and asked to be kept informed of the results. In February 1991, I wrote to request your comments on a recent Amnesty International report on "disappearances" in the Philippines, which included several cases of persons reportedly killed in the custody of security forces. In March 1991 I wrote to you and other members of the government, requesting your comments on an Amnesty International report about the extrajudicial execution of Father Narciso Pico in January.

Regrettably we have not received substantive replies to any of these letters. Amnesty International has received copies of summary reports prepared by the Commission on Human Rights (CHR) on these and other cases of human rights violations. While we certainly appreciate the CHR reports, they frequently raise more questions than they answer. They suggest, moreover, that there continue to be impediments to the proper investigation of human rights violations in the Philippines and serious weaknesses in the mechanisms for bringing the suspected perpetrators to justice. Amnesty International recently learned, for example, that the soldiers accused of responsibility for the killing of the family in Sultan Kudarat were acquitted in spite of the finding by both the CHR and the Philippines Constabulary Provincial Command, after preliminary investigation, that the killings constituted a "massacre" perpetrated by members of the 38th Infantry Battalion. This was only the latest in a series of acquittals of members of the security forces. In Amnesty International's view, it was consistent with a well established pattern in the Philippines in which members of the security forces appear to be immune from conviction for human rights related offences.

Amnesty International is deeply concerned by the failure of the government and the AFP to ensure that extrajudicial executions, and other serious violations, are thoroughly and impartially investigated and that the perpetrators are brought to justice. It believes that human rights violations such as extrajudicial executions, are likely to continue unless the perpetrators are promptly brought to justice. In failing to investigate and discipline members of its security services believed responsible for serious violations, a government creates the impression that they are above the law and in so doing condones their illegal acts.

As you may be aware, Amnesty International has in the past stated that it knows of no ranking military or police officer who has been convicted of a serious human rights related offence since the current government came to power in 1986. The government has denied this allegation but unfortunately has not yet provided Amnesty International with detailed information concerning those said to have been convicted. In 1990 the organization received from a government representative a list of some 40 police and military personnel officially said to have been convicted of human rights related offences since 1986. Amnesty International appreciated the government's effort in this regard. However, the information provided was insufficiently detailed to allow the organization to determine whether those named had in fact been convicted of human rights violations as opposed to common crimes.

I would be most grateful if your office could assist us in obtaining more detailed information about all members of the police, military and paramilitary forces who have been convicted of a serious human rights related offence since 1986. Ideally the information would include: the full name and rank of the accused; a complete description of the violation allegedly committed, including the name(s) of the victim(s) and the date and place of the incident; the venue and date of the trial proceedings; and the sentence and place of detention of the accused.

I am also writing to seek further information on a number of specific cases of apparent extrajudicial execution committed between mid-1988 and early 1990. Appended to this letter you will find a list of some 105 apparent extrajudicial executions and deaths in custody, which represent only a fraction of the cases reported to Amnesty International over the last three years.

We are interested in learning which of these cases have been the subject of investigation by the AFP or another official body, such as the National Bureau of Investigation or the Commission on Human Rights, and what the results of such investigations have been. We would also like to know whether members of the security forces have been arrested in connection with the killings listed, whether such suspects have been prosecuted and tried and, if so, whether their trials were held in military or civil courts. Of course, we would also like to be informed of the outcome of any of these trials. In the case of those convicted we would like to know what sentence or other disciplinary measure was imposed and what compensation was provided to the relatives of the victim(s). In the case of suspects acquitted, we would welcome a brief explanation of grounds for acquittal given by the courts.

Amnesty International would of course be grateful to receive copies of any supporting documents such as court decisions, witnesses' affidavits, or the published results of any official inquiries. If there is any additional information which you believe to be relevant to this matter, and which you believe will help us to reflect more accurately the position and the attitude of the government and the AFP, we would be most grateful to receive it.

I look forward to your reply,

Yours sincerely,

Ian Martin
Secretary General

☎ (44)(71) 413 5500 Telegrams: Amnesty London WC1 Telex: 28502 FAX: 956 1157

APPENDIX II

	NAME	DATE OF INCIDENT	PLACE
1.	Dante and Renate Morales	3 Jun 1988	Leyte
2.	Atty. Ramos Cura	17 Jun 1988	Pampanga
3.	Atty. Alfonso Surigao	24 Jun 1988	Cebu
4.	Atty. Emanuel Mendoza	3 Jul 1988	Manila
5.	Robert Estimada, Ferdinand Bragas	22 Jul 1988	Mountain Province
6.	Masulong Igad, Det Malugan	11 Aug 1988	South Cotabato
7.	Precy and Ruben Sabusap	1 Sep 1988	Samar
8.	Rogilio Vaflor, Jaime Vaflor	16 Sep 1988	Zamboanga del Sur Felipe Gantalao
9.	Oscar Bantayan	10 Oct 1988	Davao City
10.	Francisco Nombre	Dec 1988	Zamboanga del Sur
11.	George Bahian	30 Dec 1988	Bukinon
12.	Meliton Roxas	10 Jan 1989	Laguna
13.	Nestor Barros, Rodrigo Francisco	17 Jan 1989	Negros Occidental
14.	Sotero Soriano	23 Jan 1989	Isabela
15.	Miguel Simangon, Leopoldo Wingnga	27 Jan 1989	Kalinga-Apayao
16.	Rogelio Revilla	29 Jan 1989	Davao del Sur
17.	Remus "Boyet" Rubinos	30 Jan 1989	Bataan
18.	Marcial Ayawan	31 Jan 1989	Lanao del Norte
19.	Joel Ranis, Manuel Ranis, Alberto Pagalan, Ernesto Bernil	3 Feb 1989	Davao Oriental
20.	Semacio and Panio families	8 Feb 1989	Nueva Ecija
21.	Carmelito Anga, Rodolfo Enteron	10 Feb 1989	Davao del Sur
22.	Jimmy Boca	12 Feb 1989	Negros Occidental
23.	Eduardo Lazona	15 Feb 1989	Negros Occidental
24.	Godofredo Calaljo	18 Feb 1989	Misamis Occidental
25.	Pagao family and 4 others	19 Feb 1989	Samar
26.	Adelaida Asiong, Winnie Asiong, Narsing Nerval, Carlos Subeagan	28 Feb 1989	Aklan
27.	Romulo de la Cruz	2 Mar 1989	Samar
28.	Marcelo Dagohoy, Dikoy Flores	7 Mar 1989	Negros Occidental
29.	Serafin Pante Jr	17 Mar 1989	Quezon
30.	Jaime Sevilla	17 Mar 1989	Manila

	NAME	DATE OF INCIDENT	PLACE
31.	Atty. Oscar Tonog	21 Mar 1989	Samar
32.	Larry Duran and 6 others	22 Mar 1989	Capiz
33.	Damiano Malubay, Gervancio Cadavos	26 Mar 1989	Leyte
34.	Teodoro Egoc Sr and 4 others	29 Mar 1989	Negros Oriental
35.	Mario Boncales	5 Apr 1989	Leyte
36.	Rev. Dionisio Malalay, Rufino	6 Apr 1989	Zamboanga del Sur Rivera
37.	Diosdado Tagbar	14 Apr 1989	Cebu
38.	Carlito Arias	15 Apr 1989	Cebu
39.	Rev. Zenaido Ruelo	16 Apr 1989	Zamboanga del Sur
40.	Felix Lariosa	17 Apr 1989	Negros Occidental
41.	Ernesto Gonzales	22 Apr 1989	Negros Occidental
42.	Paombong Nine	24 Apr 1989	Bulacan
43.	Nelson Mana-ay	27 Apr 1989	Cagayan de Oro City
44.	Rev. Vizminda, Lovello Gran	1 May 1989	Misamis Occidental
45.	Freddy Grande	4 May 1989	Negros Occidental
46.	Rodolfo Vista	5 May 1989	Negros Occidental
47.	Roberto Acos, Danilo Pantonial	9 May 1989	Davao del Sur
48.	Manuel Abapo, Porferio Labayo, Bernardo Serafim	10 May 1989	Cebu City
49.	Danilo Garzo, Nelson Sabanal	22 May 1989	Negros Occidental
50.	Jury Rabaca	4 Jun 1989	Zamboanga del Sur
51.	José Eduardo Oca	8 Jun 1989	Quezon City
52.	Santiago, Buenaventura, Ruben Ramirez	10 Jun 1989	Zamboanga del Norte
53.	Gonzales Family (8)	12 Jun 1989	Agusan del Norte
54.	Emmanuel James Mabanog	14 Jun 1989	Ilocos Sur
55.	Elvis Petiluna, Alserio Baynosa, Larry Lozano	5 Jul 1989	Negros Occidental
56.	Guarina Celso and one other woman	13 Jul 1989	Northern Samar
57.	Norma Baguion	27 Jul 1989	Davao City
58.	Claudio Bucal	17 Aug 1989	Davao del Sur
59.	Rommel Moscosa	19 Aug 1989	Eastern Samar
60.	Crisostomo Ibarra	5 Sep 1989	Bataan
61.	Jacinto Manaois	2 Oct 1989	Quezon City

	NAME	DATE OF INDICENT	PLACE
62.	Ricardo Llarenas and 5 others	2 Oct 1989	Samar
63.	Edito Barcel	5 Oct 1989	Eastern Samar
64.	Jesusino Veltron, Gonzalo Lumanog	8 Oct 1989	Negros Occidental
65.	Sheila Aninon, Damian Aninon	14 Oct 1989	Cebu Dandil Dungog
66.	Jerry Ayban	25 Oct 1989	Mountain Province
67.	Candido Zafra, Edito Tabanao	8 Nov 1989	Negros Oriental
68.	Marlon Bargamente	14 Nov 1989	Negros Occidental
69.	Eulogio Sambajon and 9 others	18 Nov 1989	Camarines Sur
70.	Cornelio Limbago	15 Jan 1990	Zamboanga del Sur
71.	Diomedes Abawag	29 Jan 1990	Samar
72.	Josefina Abogada	30 Jan 1990	Zamboanga del Sur
73.	Santiago Hortilano	1 Feb 1990	Zamboanga del Sur
74.	Ruben Medina	5 Feb 1990	Bataan
75.	Wilson Leonidas	28 Feb 1990	Quezon City
76.	Oscar Tagulao	7 Mar 1990	Bataan
77.	Norman and Antonio Akien	3 Apr 1990	Mountain Province
78.	Noel Dario	6 Apr 1990	Samar
79.	Artemio Viray	16 Apr 1990	Bataan
80.	David Borja	29 Apr 1990	Iligan
81.	Cloefe Maloloy-om	3 May 1990	Cebu
82.	Edna Losanda	5 May 1990	Rizal
83.	Esperedion Calpes	24 May 1990	Negros Oriental
84.	Jose Bayotas	19 Jun 1990	Zamboanga del Sur
85.	Emelyn Lipon and others	28 Jun 1990	Bukidon
86.	Jose Dy and Gilberto Lopez	28 Jun 1990	Manila
87.	Benito Gulay	2 Aug 1990	Zamboanga del Sur
88.	Mamindiala family	3 Aug 1990	Sultan Kudarat
89.	Genaro de Guzman and 2 others	11 Aug 1990	Bataan
90.	Peralto family	16 Aug 1990	La Union
91.	Romeo Montefalcon and 4 others	29 Aug 1990	Zamboanga del Sur
92.	Noel Galain and Marquita Zimara	30 Aug 1990	Cagayan
93.	Josefina Canu	9 Sep 1990	South Cotabato

APPENDIX II

	NAME	DATE OF INCIDENT	PLACE
94.	Ferdinand Pelaro, Reynaldo de la Fuente, Aguinaldo Marfil	22 Nov 1990	Negros Occidental
95.	Perlito Lisondra	10 Dec 1990	Davao City
96.	Macario Reguma Jao	13 Dec 1990	Northern Samar
97.	Limo Arog	25 Dec 1990	South Cotabato
98.	Jose Lascano	4 Jan 1991	Manila
99.	Luisito Tesaro	7 Jan 1991	Davao City
100.	Fr. Narciso Pico	10 Jan 1991	Negros Occidental
101.	Olimpio Poso	13 Jan 1991	Samar
102.	Diosdado Evasco, Nerry Dulay	7 Feb 1991	Northern Samar
103.	Bernardo Lagurin, Miguel Calso	24 Feb 1991	Agusan del Norte
104.	Fr. Alejandro Abing	26 Feb 1991	Cebu City
105.	Emilio P. Germo	8 Mar 1991	North Cotabato

APPENDIX III

Text of CHR Chairman Bautista's 29 May 1991 letter to Amnesty International

Republika ng Pilipinas
Komisyon ng Karapatang Pantao
(Commission on Human Rights)

MCB-L-29E91-

May 29, 1991

MR. IAN MARTIN
Secretary General
Amnesty International
International Secretariat
1 Easton Street, London WC1X 8DJ
United Kingdom

Dear Mr. Martin:

I refer to your 1 May 1991 letter (Ref. TG ASA 35/91.06) expressing Amnesty International's concern about alleged extra judicial executions reportedly committed by government and government-backed troops in the Philippines since 1988.

Your letter mentioned the case of the killing of two persons during a funeral procession on 28 June 1990 allegedly by elements of security forces. The Commission has initiated a formal investigation and hearing of this case. After receiving evidence from both sides, the Commission promulgated a resolution on 17 May 1991 finding a prima facie case against the respondents and directed that the case be referred to the Prosecutor's Office of Kalookan City for the filing of the appropriate murder charges against two Philippine Constabulary officers held responsible for the killings. As regards the killing of 19 members of a Sultan Kudarat family on 3 August 1990, I regret to inform you that after a trial of the accused soldiers before General Court Martial No. 1 at which our Regional Field Officer was one of the prosecutors, the court at the conclusion of the trial and after deliberating for 3 hours, returned a verdict of not guilty and acquitted all the accused officers and enlisted personnel of both charges of murder and arson. This verdict is now final and unappealable.

On the Fr, Narciso Pico case, our investigators were able to identify one of the killers thru the testimonies of witnesses. His name was provided to the police authorities and the National Bureau of Investigation and he is expected to be apprehended any time now. We enclose a case report for your information.

As regards your concern that "Amnesty International has in the past stated that it knows of no ranking military or police officer who has been convicted of a serious human rights offence since the current government came to power in 1986", I regret that this Commission cannot provide very accurate information on this matter since all offenses of military and police personnel, with very few exceptions when court martial jurisdiction under Presidential Decree 1850 has been waived by the President, are triable by courts martial. I have therefore endorsed a copy of your letter to Defense Secretary Fidel V. Ramos for appropriate action.

As I have already stated before, this Commission is pursuing a vigorous campaign on two fronts: in the investigation of complaints for human rights violations and in the education and training of soldiers, policemen and other government personnel, and dissemination of information on the respect for, preservation and protection of human rights. I cannot overemphasize that the government's policy on human rights is unrelenting with regard to violators thereof. However, the insurgency problem in this country continues to occupy the attention of the military establishment, and this is perhaps the reason why courts martial may take longer than usual to try cases of erring military and police personnel. It may interest you to know that under the Philippine National Police law which took effect on 1 January 1991, all offenses committed by police personnel, including those committed before 1 January 1991 where the accused has not yet been formally arraigned by a court martial, are now triable by civil courts. Also, promotion in rank of military personnel require a clearance from this Commission that such candidate is not a respondent in a human rights violation case before his promotion could be effected.

We appreciate your concern regarding human rights violations in the Philippines, but your concern cannot equal that of the Philippine government and of the Philippine Commission on Human Rights in particular, since the victims are their own citizens. That there are still human rights violations occurring in the Philippines cannot be denied, but it would be difficult to totally eliminate such violations as long as the insurgency problem is extant, and where violations by both sides -- altho lately on a noticeably reduced scale -- seems to be unavoidable evil. We understand the role AI plays in exposing violations of human rights all over the world, but that role, insofar as it concerns the Philippines, must be played within the context of our own unique problems and situation. Filipinos are fiercely vigilant of their rights and they surely can find their own solution to their problems in their own original way.

Very truly yours,

MARY CONCEPCION BAUTISTA
Chairman

Encl: a/s

ESA/agb

APPENDIX IV

Excerpts from the Department of Labor and Employment's 14-page response to Amnesty International's report, *Philippines: Human Rights Violations and the Labour Movement,* June 1991 (ASA 35/16/91).

NB: The Department's response deals with a number of questions not immediately relevant to the issue of political killings. Only those sections which concern the subject matter of the current report, but are not reflected elsewhere in the text, are included here.

HUMAN RIGHTS AND THE LABOUR MOVEMENT IN THE PHILIPPINES

This paper is in response to concerns being raised by the Amnesty International over what it perceives as a continuing pattern of serious human rights violations against trade unionists in the Philippines: In a document entitled Philippines: Human Rights Violations and the Labour Movement, Amnesty International observed:

1 that trade unionists in the Philippines have been victims of serious human rights violations;

2 that the government's counter-insurgency campaign has created a condition under which violations of trade and human rights are likely to occur; and

3 that the government has persistently failed to ensure that reports of human rights violations are properly investigated and the perpetrators thereof are brought to justice.

These conclusions are based on some cases of deaths, disappearance and imprisonment
of trade union officials and members allegedly perpetrated by government, military and para-military forces. These allegations are, however, far from being conclusive. They are at best speculative and circumstantial. Misconceptions on the Government's "Total Approach" to Counter-Insurgency. Much has been said about the so-called "total approach" of government in its campaign against insurgency in the country. Some sectors claim that government's present approach is based on a package of military action involving acts of repression and violence aimed at silencing militant voices and reform oriented groups and individuals. This is, however, far from the truth. The record of the present administration speaks for itself.

After negotiations with members of the insurgency movement failed to bear fruit, the government continued pursuing initiatives in the peaceful settlement of the insurgency problem and the recognition of human and other fundamental rights in the country. The Commission on Human Rights was established along with other committees on human rights within the executive and legislative branches of government. Government's recognition of the people's inherent right to participate in political affairs was even extended to these militant groups when their political party, Partido ng Bayan [the People's Party] was recognized and continues to be recognized by the government.

For those rebels who wished to come back into the fold of the law, government also designed and is currently implementing a program for these rebels to be reintegrated back into society. Dante Buscayno, a former rebel leader who was in prison when the present government took over was released along with all other political prisoners of the past administration. Mr Buscayno received a loan from the government to enable him to set-up a cooperative movement. Countless other rebel returnees have benefitted from this program.

To ensure the delivery of basic services to people in farflung and rebel infested areas, government has, through its KABISIG program, tapped local governments and non-governmental organizations (NGOs) to implement livelihood and other socio-economic projects to combat poverty, and other socio-economic ills which have been identified as the root causes of insurgency in the country.

As can be gleaned from the foregoing, government's efforts at putting an end to the country's insurgency problem are being carried out with a high degree of compassion and political will — compassion for those who wish to come back into the fold of the law and the political will to implement political and socio-economic reforms aimed at resolving the root causes of insurgency.

Under such circumstances, it is difficult, if not impossible, for the scenario envisioned by the Amnesty International and other groups to take place. Allegations of Government Instigated or Perpetrated Violence in the Labour Movement This particular issue has reference to the alleged utilization by government of armed civilian groups to perpetrate violence and instill fear in the labor movement. Aside from being exaggerated, this allegation is also without basis.

While it is admitted that an alarming increase in the number of violent insurgent/terrorist activities since 1986 caused the proliferation of civilian voluntary organizations for community self-defense against lawless elements, the activities of these organizations have since been curtailed.

The basic State policy on organizations of such nature is found in the Constitution which provides that "the Government may call upon the people to defend the State and, in the fulfilment thereof, all citizens may be required under conditions set by law, to render personal military or civil service" (Art. II Sec. 4). It also provides in Article XVIII, Sec. 24, Transitory provisions that "private armies and other armed groups not recognized by the duly constituted authority shall be dismantled. All paramilitary forces including Civilian Home Defense Forces not consistent with the citizen armed groups established in this Constitution, shall be dissolved or, where appropriate, converted into regular forces".

It should be stressed that civilian volunteer groups were not formed nor drafted by the Government. If at all, such volunteer groups emerged out of sheer necessity of self-defense and the preservation of peace and order in the countryside, but certainly vigilantism is not a government policy. Neither does government tolerate the alleged repression of trade union rights by vigilantes.

In 1987, the following guidelines were issued for this purpose: (1) volunteer organizations shall exclusively be for self-defense and protection; (2) membership shall be purely on a voluntary basis, and thoroughly screened to week out criminal elements; (3) such organizations shall not engage in any activity contrary to law and any member who commits any offense punishable by law be prosecuted accordingly. They are also not allowed to operate offensively against the right of self-defense. A monitoring mechanism haslikewise been set-up so that the guidelines and safeguards may be carried out. In effect, the guidelines seek to ensure that civilian volunteer self-defense organizations do not commit any abuses or any acts contrary to law; that victims or complainants will be given justice and the abusers investigated and charged in court when warranted.

Other developments concerning the "vigilantes" issue in the Philippines include the following:

a.Three vigilante groups in Davao, namely Alsa Masa, Nakasaka and Tadtad were disbanded because their members have been found to be armed.

b.The Department of Local Government confiscated all firearms in the hands of unauthorized paramilitary units and vigilante groups.

c.The Philippine National Police was created to take over the enforcement of peace and order in the country, effectively excluding therefrom civilian organizations.

The "Blurring" between Legal and Illegal Opposition, Red-labelling and Other Allegations of Violence

Much ado is also being placed over efforts of government to prosecute members of outlawed organizations. While it is within the State's authority to protect its citizens against these lawless elements, some sectors have raised the issue that government has been abusing this right to curtail the free expression of human and fundamental rights. On the other hand, there are those who could see through the ploy of these elements to use trade unionism as a convenient shield against their prosecution.

This polarity in views has perhaps given rise to the perception of the Amnesty International that there seems to be a "blurring" between the legal and illegal opposition in the country such that the full exercise of the former has become imperilled as a result of government's over zealous suppression of illegal opposition. Such a view cannot be countenanced by the government. There are existing laws and institutions within the country which lay down the parameters for lawful or unlawful conduct. The exercise of legally recognized rights can never be subjected to prosecution. Unlawful acts arising therefrom must, however, contend with the full force of the law.

Thus, the exercise of the right to form and join labor organizations; to collective bargaining; and even to strike all fall within the ambit of the law. However, if in the course of the exercise of such rights, an individual commits sedition, murder, damage to property or other violent or illegal acts such individuals must face to their legal consequences. This is what happened in the cases relating to Medardo Roda, Crispin Beltran and other labor leaders during their violent welga ng bayan [national strike]. They were not brought into custody because they staged or organized the strike but because they were found to have incited sedition, an act which is punishable in almost all countries in the world.

An issue is likewise being raised against the so-called red-labelling by government forces and the peril it poses on those unfortunately labelled. The report cites as an example the military's "order of battle". It alleges that once labelled a communist, the likelihood of being extra-judicially executed increases. And yet membership in the *partido ng bayan* continues to increase. They have even manifested their intention to join future political exercises in the country. There are also a number of distinguished politicians who are known for their "communist" ideologies and sympathies such as Senator Tañada and Congressman Gillego. If there is indeed a pattern to this violence, this turn of events would not have arisen. The so-called phenomenon of red- labelling is, therefore at best speculative.

In all the specific incidents of violence of deaths cited in the report, it would be noted that there are already investigations being conducted by concerned agencies of government or, at the least, complaints have been filed with the Commission on Human Rights. In some instances, appropriate cases are already pending in court. In those cases where no such action has taken place, it would be noted that there is an absence of a complainant or an evidence to warrant the arrest and prosecution of those being accused as perpetrators.

Due process requires the presence of such complainants and evidences. While government is alarmed with the increasing resort to violence by these opposing groups, it cannot and must not prosecute these individuals based only on perceptions, speculations or baseless assumptions.

MEMORANDUM OF AGREEMENT AMONG THE COMMISSION ON HUMAN RIGHTS; THE DEPARTMENT OF NATIONAL DEFENSE, THE DEPARTMENT OF INTERIOR AND LOCAL GOVERNMENT; AND THE DEPARTMENT OF JUSTICE

The Commission on Human Rights (CHR) represented by the Honorable Chairman Mary Concepcion Bautista;

The Department of National Defense (DND) represented by the Honorable Secretary Fidel V. Ramos and the Armed Forces Chief of Staff, General Lisandro C. Abadia;

The Department of Interior and Local Government (DILG) represented by the Honorable Luis T. Santos and Philippine National Police Director General Cesar P. Nazareno; and

The Department of Justice (DOJ) represented by the Honorable Secretary Franklin M. Drilon.

WITNESSETH

WHEREAS, the General Assembly of the United Nations, in resolution 33/173 of 20 December 1978, expressed its deep concern about reports from various parts of the world relating to enforced or involuntary disappearances of persons, often while such persons were subject to detention or imprisonment;

WHEREAS, in response to this deep concern, the United Nations Commission on Human Rights decided in resolution 20 (XXXVI) of 29 February 1980 to establish the Working Group on Enforced or Involuntary Disappearances (WGEID) to investigate and inquire into clearly identified individual cases of disappearances brought to its attention by Governments, non-government and humanitarian organizations and other reliable sources;

WHEREAS, the Constitution recognizes that "all persons except those0 charged with offenses punishable by reclusion perpetua when evidence of guilt is strong, shall, before conviction, be bailable by sufficient sureties or be released on recognizance as may be provided by law.";

WHEREAS, several cases investigated by the Philippine Commission on Human Rights brought to its attention by the Working Group on Enforced or Involuntary Disappearances showed that the persons detained were allegedly released from the custody of the authorities as evidenced by documents, but that such persons immediately disappeared and were unheard from until the present;

WHEREAS, there is a need to rationalize the procedure and guidelines in the release of detainees or accused from the custody of the authorities to dispel any suspicion that the release is a mere simulation, and to clearly establish responsibility for the improper release of detainees/accused/person taken into custody;

NOW THEREFORE, the foregoing premises considered, the signatories to this Memorandum of Agreement have agreed to adopt the following procedures in the release from custody of detainees or accused persons:

1 The release of the detainee/accused/person taken into custody shall be witnessed by his spouse or adult children, or if he is unmarried or any of the foregoing are not available, by his parents, grandparents, legal guardian or other adult relatives with the detained person's approval.

2 If none of the above-mentioned relatives are available or if the detainee/accused/ person taken into custody should so choose, his release shall be witnessed by his counsel or attorney engaged by him or his relatives, or appointed by the court.

3 If none of the foregoing are available, the release of the detainee/accused/person taken into custody shall be witnessed by a representative of the CHR or any other person or persons chosen by the detainee himself.

4 In all cases, the release shall be witnessed by the Fiscal or Prosecutor having jurisdiction over the area of his detention or confinement or the judicial district where the detainee/accused/person taken into custody has been charged, or by a representative of the CHR, the parish priest, pastor, imam or religious leader, or by a well-known and respected member of the community. If the person to be released is a minor who has no parents or relatives, he shall be released to a representative of the Department of Social Welfare and Development or any charitable institution for the purpose of giving shelter and rehabilitation to said minor.

5 All releases must be made evidenced by a document that must state clearly the name of the detainee/accused/person taken into custody, the exact date and time of his release, the printed name and signature of the person or persons receiving his living body indicating relationship, if any, to the detainee/accused/person taken into custody, and the independent witness, and the custodian, all of whom must sign over the printed names in the document, with specific designation of their position, rank, unit or office, as the case may be.

6 The prison warden, jail warden, precinct commander, detachment headquarters commander or the head of the unit or office, or any authorized person having custody of the detainee/accused/person taken into custody shall maintain within the premises a separate official logbook — notwithstanding the existence of a police blotter or any other official logbook required for other purposes — that shall indicate therein the names of all persons arrested or brought in and detained, the name of the person arresting or bringing him in, the time and date of his arrival at the premises of his detention, the reason for his detention, and the time and date of his release and other circumstances thereof. Such official logbook shall be open for perusal by the relatives, friends, lawyer of the detained person, and to the general public.

7 Where detainee/accused/person taken into custody is reportedly released from hiscustodians or captors in the manner not confirming to the foregoing procedure, and such detainee/accused/person taken into custody thereafter disappears or is found dead, the burden is on his custodians/captors to prove that the missing person was released safely, or that the foregoing procedure for his release was in fact observed and duly witnessed.

8 It shall be the responsibility of the prison warden, jail warden, precinct commander,detachment headquarters commander, camp commander or the head of the unit or office, or any authorized person having custody of the detainee/accused/person taken into custody to see to it that the foregoing procedures are strictly observed and enforced. Failure to observe the foregoing procedures shall make the warden, commander or unit head, together with the custodians and captors or persons concerned liable for administrative or penal sanctions as provided by law.

9 For purposes of this Memorandum of Agreement, the foregoing provisions shall apply to all cases of detention, arrests, apprehension and invitations for custodial investigations.

Done this 18th day of June 1991 in the Year of Our Lord, in Pasig, Metro Manila.

MARY CONCEPCION BAUTISTA
Chairman
Commission on Human Rights

FRANKLIN M. DRILON
Secretary
Department of Justice

FIDEL V. RAMOS
Secretary
Department of National Defense

LUIS T. SANTOS
Secretary
Department of Interior and Local Government

GENERAL LISANDRO C. ABADIA
Chief of Staff
Armed Forces of the Philippines

CESAR P. NAZARENO
Director General
Philippine National Police

WITNESSES:

SAMUEL J. SORIANO
Commissioner
Commission on Human Rights

HESIQUIO R. MALLILLIN
Commissioner
Commission on Human Rights

NARCISO C. MONTEIRO
Commissioner
Commission on Human Rights

PAULYNN PAREDES SICAM
Commissioner
Commission on Human Rights

BRIG. GEN. EMILIANO D. TEMPLO
Deputy Chief of Staff for
Senior State Prosecutor
Armed Forces of the Philippines

FISCAL NILO C. MARIANO
Civil-Military Operations
Department of Justice

MARCIANO I. BACALLA
Chief, Human Rights Division
Department of National Defense